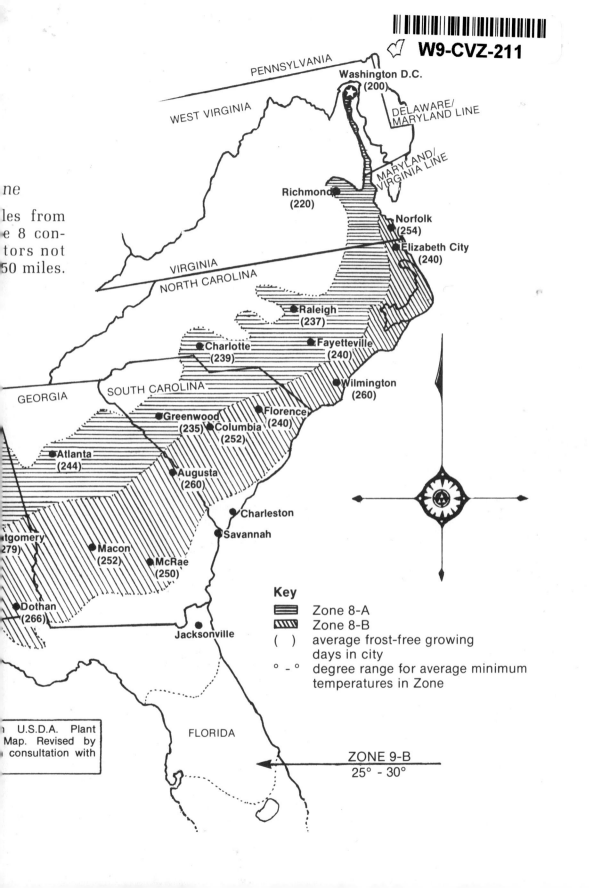

PENNSYLVANIA

Washington D.C.
(200)

WEST VIRGINIA

DELAWARE/
MARYLAND LINE

MARYLAND/
VIRGINIA LINE

Richmond
(220)

Norfolk
(254)

Elizabeth City
(240)

VIRGINIA
NORTH CAROLINA

ne

les from
e 8 con-
tors not
50 miles.

Raleigh
(237)

Charlotte
(239)

Fayetteville
(240)

SOUTH CAROLINA

Wilmington
(260)

GEORGIA

Greenwood
(235)

Florence
(240)

Columbia
(252)

Atlanta
(244)

Augusta
(260)

Charleston

Savannah

tgomery
279)

Macon
(252)

McRae
(250)

Dothan
(266)

Jacksonville

Key

▤ Zone 8-A

▨ Zone 8-B

( ) average frost-free growing
days in city

° - ° degree range for average minimum
temperatures in Zone

U.S.D.A. Plant
Map. Revised by
consultation with

FLORIDA

ZONE 9-B
25° - 30°

Fred Heutte's
Gardening
in the
Temperate Zone

Fred Heutte's
Gardening
in the
Temperate Zone

By Frederic Heutte

Edited by Betsy Trundle

With an introduction by
Dr. John L. Creech, *Director*
U.S. National Arboretum

Donning

Illustrations and cover art
  by Debbi Pillar

Library of Congress Cataloging in Publication Data

Heutte, Frederic, 1899-
Fred Heutte's Gardening in the Temperate Zone.

Bibliography: p.
Includes index.
1. Gardening—Southern States. I. Title.
II. Title: Gardening in the Temperate Zone.
SB453.2.S66H48   635.9'0975   77-11096
ISBN 0-915442-35-3

To Florence
who has sustained my efforts
over the past 53 years
of our marriage

Contents

Introduction

Fred Heutte can be called a gardener's gardener, for the wide respect that his long and intimate association with plants in the garden setting has earned him. Coming up through the demanding school of estate gardening when perfection was expected, Mr. Heutte became supervisor of the Norfolk City parks in 1937. He continued to beautify the City of Norfolk until 1958 when he was appointed Director of the Norfolk Botanical Gardens at which post he remained until his retirement in 1966.

Shortly after I arrived in Washington in 1947, I became acquainted with Fred Heutte through his interest in testing plant introductions. I can recall visiting his tidal-water site where he expounded on the response of several plants to brackish water. At the same time, he was utilizing a mist system on tall stand pipes to create a suitable environment for broadleaved evergreens. Interest in and love for azaleas and camellias have been highlights of Mr. Heutte's career. The collections of these remarkable plants in the Botanical Gardens as well as throughout Norfolk are a tribute to his pioneer efforts.

A long admirer of Tidewater Virginia and thoroughly at home with growing plants under these favorable conditions, Mr. Heutte has shared this knowledge of plants in *Gardening In The Temperate Zone*. He prepared the book in a style that would lose its character if his manner of relating his experiences were altered. In a sense, this book is a picture of Mr. Heutte's personality as well as his intimate understanding of plants.

Mr. Heutte has assembled a month-by-month journal of the annual parade of plants in Temperate Zone 8 and an in-depth commentary which reveals his special capabilities in working with plants. As a result, the reader will find many "tips" on better gardening that only could come from one so well-versed in the particular demands of each plant discussed. While Mr. Heutte has written from experience based in Tidewater Virginia, there are so many basic facts applicable to all of us who garden in the temperate zone, the book will remain a useful working tool to fine gardening for future generations of gardeners.

John L. Creech
Washington, D.C.

Foreword

Gardening In The Temperate Zone is the culmination of my sixty-three years involvement with gardening, both as a vocation and avocation. It would be the fulfillment of a life-long dream if the contents lead its readers to a better understanding of what a great contribution the average home garden can make towards a more beautiful world. And I am also hopeful that my experience and knowledge can benefit the people of Tidewater, Virginia, who, over the past forty years, have sustained my efforts to develop public areas and gardens, some of which have attained national recognition.

My career has given me particular knowledge of the climate and growing conditions that exist in the southeastern area of this country as designated by the A and B sections of our Zone 8 map, which was adapted from the Plant Hardiness Map produced by the United States Department of Agriculture. I have abbreviated the original map to exclude the more arid areas and include only the portions that have a fairly uniform rainfall and an average temperature that rarely varies ten degrees in its severity on the low side. The notation of the growing days in the twenty-five different sections of the map, covering parts of eight states, will allow readers to relate the text of the book to their area as the time schedule is for an average growing season, and blooming schedules and gardening chores do vary even in so defined an area as our zone.

While the geographical limitations of this book do not preclude its use beyond the confines of the map, they do allow me to present specific and accurate descriptions of the plant species that prevail within its borders, although it will always be the exotic plants that offer the greatest challenge to those who find gardening a thrilling adventure.

I do not claim to have written an encyclopedia of gardening but rather a chronicle of the plants which I have loved the best. They include many species that are climatically compatible to our zone but rarely found in gardens as they have not attracted the attention of the nursery trade. Since I believe that timing and sequence are the main ingredients in good gardening and landscaping, the plants are listed in chronological order as they appear at their best. All varieties described in the book grow well in our zone.

It is my hope that in the Diary section amateurs and professionals alike will enjoy the floral parade that has so intrigued me all these years and surprises me still. In the work schedule I have included the monthly chores that my experience as a practical gardener has shown me to be the most essential. In these pages you will find all the knowledge that I have gleaned from my predecessors, associates and amateur gardeners in Tidewater, and the information that I have tracked down whenever an unusual plant attracted my attention.

Certain plant species and aspects of gardening are of such special interest to me, and apparently to others, that I have devoted individual chapters to them. In particular, the Camellia species has always ranked first in my affection for the plant kingdom and initiated much of my research and travel throughout our zone. It has always distressed me to see how seldom they are grown since they are outstanding performers in our area, which has rightfully been called Camellia country.

I have refrained from being too specific about spraying and insect control because it has become so technical that it tends to confuse the average gardener. The United States Department of Agriculture is exercising such control over the manufacture and distribution of insecticides that the surest way to an effective spray program is through your local Agricultural Agent.

At seventy-nine I present this book to share my love of gardening and will close with the philosophy of Aristotle that has been a guiding principle in my life's career: "Nature has the will but not the power to reach perfection."

Fred Heutte

A Gardener's Diary

January

The gateway to winter, January is our coldest month. Even in the most temperate areas of our coverage, this cold and gusty month affects plant behavior and challenges the best of gardeners, for in January, the average is a rarity; most days are either much colder or warmer, although the rainfall is usually sufficient for your garden's needs. The weather is only one of the unpredictable elements in gardening, and in the following chapters I not only want to share with you my knowledge of horticulture but help you enjoy and deal with the many surprises that make gardening such an exciting pastime. For sixty-three years my life has been plants and gardening, and I am still finding new experiences and discoveries to capture my enthusiasm.

Hollies

Looking out my window on the chilled January landscape, I think of my garden as a stage, and take particular pride in the rugged Hollies, whose bright berries outperform all other evergreens at this time of the year.

There are many more Hollies than I will mention here; in fact, there are over a thousand varieties listed in the trade. I would rather not confuse you with hundreds of names but excite your curiosity about the characteristics of the different Hollies, so that you might explore the possibilities and select those best suited for your environment. We are now entering a new year, so even if you have limited space, make room for at least one Holly.

However, should you plant a solitary specimen, it should be within one quarter of a mile of others, either in the wild or nearby in a neighbor's yard. Hollies are in most part "dioecious," which means that the male and female flowers are on separate plants (staminate and pistillate) and must be cross-pollinated by wind currents or bees to bear fruit. But don't be alarmed if your new Holly does not berry well the first year, or if old shrubs seem to have bare seasons, as it is perfectly normal for most Hollies to berry heavily on alternate years. While I don't want to bore you with technical details, this initial explanation should suffice to guide you in dealing with all plants whose main landscape feature is fruit. In these cases cross-pollinization occurs in the spring when the flowers are in bloom; and for maximum berry production Hollies should not be pruned until after their blooming season, which varies with the species.

The entire family of Hollies is fascinating, but if I could select only one, it would be the Lusterleaf Holly, *Ilex latifolia*, which you would not even recognize as a Holly except at this time of the year when it produces a long cluster of red berries. This magnificent specimen is from China and Japan, and grows to thirty feet tall and one-third as broad with six inch leaves, one-half inch wide. But for the red berries, one quarter of an inch in diameter, the spineless leaves would make the tree look more like a small evergreen Magnolia than a Holly. For its greatest performance it should be allowed to grow unhampered to the ground and given spreading space at least ten feet in diameter. Even out of berry it stands out as one of the most beautiful evergreens.

Of course, the American Holly, *Ilex opaca,* is much hardier and equally as beautiful if you are able to cope with the Holly Leaf Miner, a pesky insect that requires a good spraying program.

Many Holly hybrids have been developed from the English and Oriental Hollies, and my long-lasting favorite is Nellie Stevens, a cross between a Chinese and an English Holly. Nellie grows to thirty feet or more in a pyramidal form and berries consistently year after year with no sparse season. Its main characteristics are its spiney foliage and two inch long berry clusters which do not appeal to birds' appetites, therefore enhancing your garden long after other berries have been devoured. It is one of the Hollies that bears flowers while still in berry and will take any temperature covered by our Zone 8 map and beyond.

Those living along the coast and exposed to windswept areas would want to use the Youpon Holly, *Ilex vomitoria.* This is the Holly that southeastern tribes of American Indians held in reverence because the tea brewed from its tiny leaves confirmed their health, restored their appetites, and gave them courage and agility in war. We do not need them for that purpose, but do admire the profusion of bright berries they produce early in the season.

The Youpons are native along the coast from southern Virginia to Florida and grow to twenty-five feet. They multiply through underground runners, often creeping out onto the sandy beaches of the coast where, buffeted by high winds and tides, they will stand as a protecting hedge for other shore vegetation.

Nellie Stevens. National Arboretum photo.

The Youpon's growth habits lend the shrubs to close shearing and make them ideal hedges and subjects for topiary. In the Palace Gardens of Colonial Williamsburg they have been used as substitutes for Boxwood.

Dwarf varieties of Youpon are available in the trade, and, though shy of the usual heavy berry clusters, are invaluable as small hedges of no more than four feet. It is even possible to find weeping varieties of the Youpon, making this hardy Holly one of our

Weeping Youpon Holly, *Ilex vomitoria.*

Youpon Holly topiary

most versatile.

If you are looking for dwarf evergreens, the many varieties of the black-berried Japanese Holly, *Ilex crenata,* are equally as versatile as the Youpon and more readily available. Most varieties are small, such as *I. helleri,* which grows only two feet, and *I. microphylla,* even more dwarf with tiny leaves and ideally suitable for foundation planting in proximity to dwellings. The Japanese Hollies are hardy beyond the limits of our map and come in so many varieties that a visit to your local nursery is sometimes necessary to select plants which best suit your purpose.

Many members of the Holly family have invaded our areas from the north and lend great charm to our winter gardens. Of these, I would recommend the smooth Winterberry, *Ilex laevigata,* most often seen in swampy areas, although it grows well on high ground. Found from Maine to Georgia, the Winterberry is not an evergreen, but the orange-red fruit, borne singly along the tips of the stems, have won it a permanent place in our landscape. *Ilex decidua* is another deciduous Holly offered by the trade for those of you who want to add the unusual to your garden. Because these Hollies lose their leaves in the autumn, the berries, with no competition from the foliage, are more intense and truly outstanding.

As you can see, the uses of Hollies are almost unlimited. I have mentioned among the resources a book which will acquaint you with more varieties and help you in your selection. My own Holly garden is a great pleasure to me, and never fails to surprise visitors with the wide range in size and appearance of my trees and shrubs. This garden not only provides indoor decoration, but I always stick a few sprigs of Holly in my window boxes, where the quickly maturing berries attract the birds.

Whatever use you choose for your Hollies, either as a two foot ground cover, or a fifty foot tree, nothing brightens up the winter landscape like a "Holly-berry-parade." With the hundreds of varieties and hybrids now available in commercial nurseries, all gardeners should be able to find several to suit their tastes.

The Japanese Anise Tree

One of my favorite evergreens is the Japanese Anise Tree, *Illicium anisatum,* which I was fortunate enough to come across many years ago and plant in my garden. The texture of the foliage makes it very decorative, and you will not believe your eyes when you see it in bloom on the freezing days of January. You might guess that it is used in the French liqueur by the same name. The Anise Tree is also valued for its leaves, which are quite aromatic when crushed and are often used in Oriental cooking.

This evergreen will eventually grow to fifteen feet and in full vigor will flower every January. The blooms are not spectacular; they are extremely small, white, semi-double flowers with a yellowish cast, but they are fascinating to watch as they pop out from day to day, even as the temperature hovers around the freezing point.

I warn you that the Japanese Anise Tree is not common, for propagation is difficult, and, to my knowledge, can only be achieved through layering.

Anise Tree, *Illicium anisatum,* in my garden.

However, it is worth looking for since its lustrous foliage and unusual blooming habits make it quite a conversation piece.

Camellias

Although many Camellias bloom throughout the winter months, there is one star of the January landscape, Lady Clare, *Camellia japonica*. This old and most reliable Camellia will bloom at the proverbial drop of a hat if it has been carefully planted with some protection from the strong cold winds and the early sun rays from the east, which may thaw the frozen blossoms too rapidly.

However, it should be noted that the same variety planted in Richmond or Washington, D. C., would not dare to expand its flower buds until possibly mid-February or March. Therefore, while we indicate this variety as hardy, like all *Camellia japonica* species, the lines on our map denoting growing days will help you determine their blooming period in your particular locale.

To emphasize the time lapse enjoyed by Camellias, I would like to point out the differing show dates

Lady Clare Camellia, *Camellia japonica*.

along the East Coast, for they indicate the average peak flowering period of those areas. The most southern penetration for Camellias is in Louisiana, with a show date of mid-December. Washington, D. C., is normally last on the show circuit in mid-April. Norfolk, Virginia, usually has show dates in late March and Fayetteville, North Carolina, in mid-February. It is also interesting to note that each year the same varieties will, on average, win the top awards in all the areas.

Heaths and Heathers

Large shrubs are not alone in giving interest and color to the winter landscape. Heaths (*Erica*) and Heathers (*Calluna*) are low-growing evergreens that will bloom in the fall and spasmodically in our coldest month.

Heaths and heathers do not grow in our representative climate by choice and are a challenge to grow; but they will tolerate our hot summers if grown in an environment that will deflect the hot southern sun rays that prevent adequate moisture and are detrimental to their well-being. Soil conditions also play an important part in their survival. It is essential that they have an acid soil, as opposed to alkaline, with a range between pH 5.0 and pH 5.5. This is a condition that must be derived through the addition of peat moss or leaf mold and not by chemicals. Heaths and Heathers are most at home on the English moor, and do not like rich fertile soil. Unlike most plants, they will resent the addition of fertilizer and do much better for you in soil that is not cultivated.

The varieties of Heath that are most tolerant of our summer heat are Springwood Pink and Springwood

White. They will bloom from late winter to early spring and are recommended for anyone who may be challenged to grow them.

The Christmas and Lenten Rose

Other invaders from the north are the Christmas and Lenten Rose, *Helleborus orientalis* and *Helleborus atrorubens.* Thriving in damp, shaded areas in deep, peaty soil, these leaf-losing perennials are ideal for a winter woodland setting. Their main idiosyncrasy is their resentment of frequent transplanting. Therefore, before planting them, carefully select permanent areas with well-drained soil and await their appearance, perhaps in mid-January along the coast or mid-February inland.

Christmas Roses are purchased as dormant roots and should be planted in the fall or early spring. Protect the plants with adequate mulch, preferably hardwood leaves such as oak, which will furnish acid plant food as it disintegrates.

What a thrill to await their arrival! The delicate purple blossoms resemble the old-fashioned Rose and grow on plants ten to twelve inches high. The masses of dark leaves generally disappear before the flowers bloom, making their show all the more exciting. What a wonderful plant for the wild garden.

Italian Arum

From time to time those of us who collect plants for a hobby will discover some that are hard to track down unless properly identified at the onset. Such was the Italian Arum, which I generally recognized as a member of the Jack-in-the-Pulpit family, and erroneously classified as an *Arisaema,*

Italian Arum, *Arum italicum.*

the beautiful wild flower of our eastern states, which dies down during the winter. This nomad in my garden proved to be *Arum italicum,* which produces a rather insignificant Jack-in-the-Pulpit bloom in the late spring, but in the fall presents a beautiful cluster of bright red fruit on the same spathe, which is also its source of distribution.

The main feature of the Italian Arum is its large, lance-shaped green foliage which persists during the coldest winter months. Truly nomadic, it will appear at various emplacements in the yard, seemingly seeking damp, shaded areas. At this time of the year it is unique, especially on a frosty morning.

Palms

What could be more startling and exotic than the silhouette of a Palm Tree in a snowstorm? Although a challenge to grow in the northern extremes of our area, a few varieties are resistant to cold winters. One of these is the Windmill Palm, *Trachycarpus fortunei,* one of the fan Palms. There is a twenty-foot tree which has survived more than forty winters as far north as the Norfolk Botanical Gardens. So for the touch of the tropical, they are worth trying in our area.

Man-made micro-climates not only extend the season of hardy plants, but allow you to grow many specimens not generally considered possible for our area. There are several ways in which to emulate Mother Nature's more favorable climates.

One of the oldest methods of building a micro-climate, and especially appealing to gardening innovators, is the construction of a pit. First, locate an area alongside your home, or a wall that has a southern exposure, then dig a large hole three to four feet below ground level so that it will be below the frost line. Construct a lean-to six to seven feet high and finish it off with a transparent lid of any light-filtering material. Plexiglass is actually preferable to glass since it won't break. Make certain that you ventilate your pit with windows or doors on the east and west sides of your construction. Now let your imagination sparkle at all the tropical plants you can grow. George Washington used just such a contraption at Mount Vernon and grew orange trees in it. He later equipped it with a flue, which he kept heated with wood.

Another method is to enclose a courtyard with solid masonry walls. Open to the sky, your private garden will allow you to grow semi-tropical plants where only temperate ones would have grown before your alteration.

Your foundation shrubs can also become insulators for more tender plants if you place them four feet away from your home's southern exposure. Your heated home, blocking the cold air from the north, warms this small pocket, and you can use it to bring Daffodils to flower weeks ahead of schedule or to winter over such plants as the Shrimp Plant and Begonias, which would normally not survive.

In the Tidewater area, where the tidal lands are cut up by many rivers and bodies of water, micro-climates are ever present. Richmond, Raleigh, and Atlanta have hills and valleys that create climate differentials within a few miles of each other. Every terrain, whether through natural topography or man-made improvements, will have micro-climates of differing degrees. These are the conditions which allow your neighbor to grow certain plants that just won't do a thing in your own garden. Perhaps you say, "Why not grow only the plants that I know are hardy?" That may be acceptable to some, but I think most average gardeners enjoy exploring a medley of plants and thrill at the discovery of that singular plant which will uniquely thrive in their particular settings. In the following pages I am going to describe many plants that grow in Zone 8, but with emphasis on those odd little creatures that pop up now and then, defying everyone's preconceptions about what will grow in our climate.

While gardening is not at a complete standstill, January does offer us free time to dream a little of ways to improve our gardens by either selecting new plants or moving those we already have. It is a time to contemplate our world of beauty in which all things that grow play an important role.

January Work Schedule

To accomplish the most in the home garden, we must take advantage of every opportunity presented by those occasional temperate days in January when we can work with comfort and still be within the time schedules best suited for the plants involved.

Pruning

One of the first chores that comes to mind is pruning, and you should probably start with Rose canes. Since winter winds tend to whip Rose canes about and loosen their root systems, January is the time to remove about one-half of their previous year's growth for plants three feet tall or taller. Climbers should be tied back to their supports; this is not the proper time for their annual pruning.

Grape vines bleed readily when pruned later than February or March. Although severe bleeding will not be fatal, January pruning tends to conserve their strength and, more importantly, lightens our work load in the busy season ahead.

Growing Grapes is tricky if you are not familiar with their many idiosyncracies, but many bulletins are available through county agricultural agents to assist you in their culture. They not only illustrate proper pruning techniques but list the proper varieties to plant for your area. Under proper management Grapes can be a satisfying and economic crop.

This is also the time to obtain free bulletins on fruit trees, whether you plan to prune established trees or contemplate purchasing new ones. Dwarf forms of most fruiting trees are now available and are an excellent choice for many home gardens. To help in your selection and for your reading pleasure, send for a free catalog from Stark Brothers. However, the final selection of fruit trees should be guided by your county agent or local authority. Few garden subjects are as responsive as fruit to varied climatic conditions, which dictate which variety will outperform another within only a few miles distance.

One of the few ornamentals that requires January pruning is the Sasanqua Camellia, which flowers in the fall and will now be all bloomed out. This is more or less in keeping with the good practice of pruning a plant after it flowers. Guidelines for pruning other varieties of this genus are described in the chapter on Camellias.

One of the most timely chores for winter work is dormant spraying, which is consistently emphasized by experimental stations and professionals. A dormant spray is a spray applied to a dormant plant, which hosts

January Rose pruning.

over-wintering insects such as scale, spider mites, and even aphids.

Most fruit trees benefit from an application of dormant oil spray after pruning. Hence Apple, Pear, Peach, and Cherry Trees should be included in this month's schedule, with certain precautions. Foremost among these is attention to the temperature. The spray must be applied when the thermometer rises above forty-five degrees and is due to stay there for the next twenty-four hours.

There are several formulas of dormant sprays, some of miscible oils and others of lime-sulphur. It is imperative that you inquire from reliable sources the type and dilution best suited for your problem.

Sanitation is important in your garden for much more than appearance's sake. We must be reminded that many insects, and some diseases, over-winter in garden debris, and it becomes imperative to remove this litter in order to eliminate a future breeding place or beachhead of unwanted problems.

Most of the garden chores are elementary and require only good common sense. For instance, the slack month of January is the perfect time to clean and sharpen your garden tools, with lawn-mowing equipment heading the list.

For the most part January gardeners spend more time in their armchairs than out of doors. These chilly days are perfect for planning your spring garden and perusing some of the better gardening catalogs. One of the best is put out by Wayside Gardens, long recognized as the sophisticated encyclopedia for better perennials and other plants. It is also well illustrated in color and worth the price of one dollar.

As with most priced catalogs, the cost is reimbursable upon purchase of mechandise.

Gardening, especially during our leisure moments, should be inspirational and this can best be accomplished through the reading of good books. In my case I have read and re-read *This Green World* by Rutherford Platt. It does not deal with the growing of plants, but rather with their physical development and insight into the mystery of plant life itself. This would be the last book I would dispose of from my library shelf. If I might suggest another, it would be *The Story of Gardening* by Richardson Wright. It, too, will inspire you with the story of the progress of gardening from the Hanging Gardens of Babylon to the Hanging Gardens of New York. As you digest these two books, you will appreciate your garden more, for you will better understand that wonderful partner we call nature.

February

Interesting gardens are those which from time to time present an element of surprise, and February at its best is not conducive to producing many. But if we concentrate our search we'll find a few plants which are most exciting in the winter landscape.

I came across a February performer some years ago with the pretty name Star Flower, *Tritelia uniflora*. This gem, a native of western America, adapts so well in our area that it escapes cultivation and grows wild.

The Star Flower originates from a small bulb and grows six to eight inches tall. The pale lilac flowers, which last forty to sixty days, commence blooming in the warmer areas in early February, but self-regulate themselves according to our zone. Because they are extremely hardy, you may see them peeping out just as the snow begins to melt. What a surprise! The bulbs are so inexpensive that you can afford a hundred or more. Plant them in the fall about six inches apart in a shaded area of well-loosened peaty soil. Anytime after the first of the year the Star Flower's foliage will appear, looking like so much grass until ready to bloom. Following their flower show they soon disappear until the next year, by which time they will have doubled. They go underground in their search for new pastures and can penetrate hard-packed sod paths that may border their original home. Such is the life of the Star Flower, always pushing on to spring a surprise where you least expect it.

Fragrance is an attribute always sought in the garden, but is really a novelty when it permeates the winter landscape. Offering just such a treat is Winter-Sweet, *Chimonanthus praecox* or *Meratia praecox,* not a rare plant but uncommon in the average garden. This perfectly hardy shrub prefers open sunlight to light shade, and will eventually grow eight to nine feet. Borne along naked stems, the flowers are creamy yellow around a quarter-of-an-inch in diameter with reddish brown centers. Winter-Sweet leaves no doubt about when it is in bloom; the profusion of flowers spreads their delightful fragrance everywhere. And they can be brought indoors since the two to three foot stems make it a natural for flower arranging. We are indebted to China for this wonderful plant.

Winter-Sweet, *Chimonanthus praecox,*
National Arboretum photo.

The name Daphne has been associated with beautiful things since Greek mythology, and in the realm of the plant world it is the most fragrant. There are quite a few species but the earliest to bloom is *Daphne odora.* Like so many plants that bloom at this time of the year, the *Daphne odora,* though classified as tender, has been found to thrive in colder regions if afforded some protection. First of all, it prefers a semi-shaded location, but much more important, an extremely well-drained soil. When planting Daphne add one-half sand and one-half loam, omitting all chemical additives. During dry periods the loam will help keep the soil moist, which is necessary for the plant. A good thick mulch of pine needles aids in this and will give the soil all the acidity required. Failure to observe these precautions will doom it to an early failure.

Other Daphnes will be mentioned in their proper blooming sequence. *Daphne odora* is a slow grower to two feet with equal spread and should be protected well the first year. It is easily propagated in the summer.

Another surprise which nature often provides in her will-of-the-wisp manner is the appearance of early

Daphne, *Daphne odora.*

spring-blooming Crocus. In my own yard, over many years, the species *Tomasinianus* almost always heralds the coming of spring. This pale lavender flower, with silver-gray outline, long ago escaped its original setting under a Camellia bush and sought greener pastures, pushing through hard sod and spreading its progeny in all directions. Such personalities of the plant world command respect and come at their own bidding, keeping no set schedule. Each February I await the arrival of my Crocus and know their welcome means spring will soon be here in spite of what the calendar tells me.

Try some of the planted Crocus which are quite inexpensive and offered by bulb specialists. They were originally collected in the wild and are sold as mixed species, not varieties as is often the case with bulbs. When your Crocus surprise you by blooming in

unsuspected places, spare them from mowing until the foliage disappears, which means that they have matured and gone underground to greet you another cold February day the following year.

February Work Schedule

Even in the warmer areas covered by this book, February is not an ideal month to work in the garden. Yet wherever we may live nature is slowly awakening from its hibernation.

Insect Control

The first stirrings of spring often take place in the insect world, such as over-wintering egg masses that lay within the upper folds of the earth or along the crevices of some fruit trees, just waiting to hatch and forage again on their favorite host plants. The strange metamorphosis of nature that triggers off insects is still a puzzle to scientists. Yet we know that no matter what the weather presents, insects awake at the right time to forage on their favorite food. Tent caterpillars are a perfect example of scales which remain hidden and camouflaged until hatched.

Tent Caterpillars must be
curbed before migration.

If you were unable to use a dormant oil spray in January, make sure that you do so this month. If you wait as late as March 15 to apply your spray, the dilution must be greater, as directions on the can will indicate, especially as applied to Roses.

Dormant oil applications do not control all insects, but check many, such as aphids, mites, and certain scales, at their source. Just visualize, if you will, the potential problem of insects which, if not stopped, will multiply in some instances a hundred-fold once hatched and in some species, continue as a weekly process.

Soil Preparation

The success of any garden depends in great measure on the condition of the soil for root penetration, and the mere breaking up of six inches is not sufficient. The soil must be prepared and conditioned at least fifteen inches in depth for raising seeds or seedlings.

From farmers we learn that the earlier we start this process, the better the crops. But whatever our time

schedule, aeration of the packed soil is a good tonic, and some even claim that it is equivalent to the application of fertilizer as it allows the nitrogen and other elements in the soil to reach the air, which activates the micro-organisms.

Roto-tillers are becoming more and more popular for home soil preparation, and can be rented from hardware stores. However, many gardeners will rely on the old-fashioned method of spading the ground by hand. This sounds like a back-breaking job, but I have a system which allows me to work at my own pace, doing only the work that I feel comfortable doing in a day. My secret is to plan my work so that I have only to do a small section a day, such as 250 square feet, which I can work in an hour.

Before digging any garden plot we must determine what additives are necessary to bring the soil to the proper nutrient value needed for what we plan to grow. This is best done by taking a soil test to the nearest soil-testing laboratory. To take a soil test,

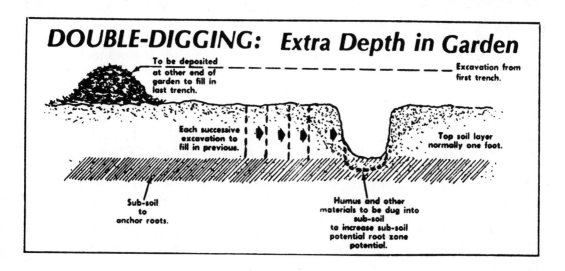

DOUBLE-DIGGING: Extra Depth in Garden

To be deposited at other end of garden to fill in last trench.

Excavation from first trench.

Each successive excavation to fill in previous.

Top soil layer normally one foot.

Sub-soil to anchor roots.

Humus and other materials to be dug into sub-soil to increase sub-soil potential root zone potential.

dig six trowels full of soil, taken at random at least ten feet apart, then mix them thoroughly. From this extract one trowel and place it in a milk carton or other disposable container and take it for analysis.

Once we know what is needed in our garden, we are ready to prepare the soil. I define the area that I wish to improve and dig my first spadeful at one end of my garden, depositing it at the outer edge of the area I intend to prepare. I then dig a trench of at least fifteen inches deep across the width of my planned garden. Into this trench I put at least one inch of humus and the needed additives, refilling it with the soil from the trench that I make immediately adjacent. This way I can do as small or as large an area as I like, and the fluffed layer of soil that I create is ideal for root penetration. By using this method we can develop a deep, rich topsoil, exposing some of the sub-soil to the surface and incorporating a form of humus each year. Try it; you will benefit from the exercise as well as the results.

Pruning

While some pruning may have been accomplished on favorable January days, it becomes a must during February and mid-March, especially for fruit trees. Where Fig trees are prevalent, they should head the list since they are prone to bleeding. Here again, let me recommend the free bulletins available on this subject at county agents. We prune fruit trees to increase quality so that each fruit can become the Apple of your eye. The process must involve removing all surplus and injured limbs, leaving an open-headed tree which allows the sunlight to penetrate. This pruning

Open-headed tree after pruning to allow air circulation.

results in fewer fruit of higher quality.

Starting Seedlings

Even without the advantage of a greenhouse or sun porch, we can anticipate spring by sowing seeds in February. Especially successful are those of slow germination and maturity such as Begonias, Impatiens, and Petunias.

Seedlings are particularly easy to grow through the use of modern innovations such as indoor greenhouses. Two feet by two feet and eighteen inches high, these greenhouses come complete with wick-fed automatic watering trays and cost less than twenty-five dollars. At an additional cost they can be fitted with fluorescent lights and a timer. Their capacity will readily accommodate up to five hundred seedlings, which can be planted in trays or pots of sterilized starter mixtures to ready them for the outdoors. Without lights, the greenhouse goes on a sunny window sill for a head start on spring. What a wonderful modern innovation.

You might also investigate the great strides that have been made in the manufacture of outdoor cold frames. When equipped with automatic electric heating cables, and in some cases automatic ventilators, they are far superior to the old-fashioned hot-beds which were heated through the fermentation of animal manures. Not only can you start your spring garden early, but just think of picking fresh and crisp lettuce all winter long.

A simple cold frame.

March

The awakening of a gentle giant might well describe this calendar month, and as we bend our ear to listen to the earthly bosom, we hear the pulsating sounds of renewed activity. The boring of the earthworm slowly grinds up soil particles, which when digested and deposited above the ground, make up our good earth. The tunneling mole silently seeks the grubs that may later destroy our crops. The ricochetting overhead of the early pollen grains from the Maple blossoms heralds the time to sow our early crops. These are but a few whispers in the wind—the promise that spring is soon to arrive.

I often wondered why March was my favorite month, until I realized that I first saw the light of day within its fold, on St. Joseph's day, to be exact, March 19. This day marks the end of frost warnings for my area, and the Camellia world touches our heart strings with its multitude of blossoms, surrounded by a carpet of the last of the early Crocus, blended with Daffodils.

We wonder at the prolificacy of the Chickweed so genteel in its progress until we realize that it is overtaking our Pansies and Violets and other har-bingers of spring. We then realize that we must stop dreaming and muster our resources to guard the wonders that

Spring comes to Zone 8.

nature has placed in our trust, especially the weaker ones which mantle
our earth, such as the perennial Candytuft, *Iberis sempervirens,* which is
glistening white, especially the newer
varieties, Snowmantle and Purity.

Wherever the ground is poor,
Carpet Phlox, *Phlox subulata,* may
take over with dazzling colors of red,
blue, white, rose, and purple. Yes,
impoverished soil will suit them along
dry banks and fallow fields because
nature has willed that our gardens
must be served.

Consider a Johnny-jump-up such
as *Viola kitaibeliana,* the wild one, for
the shady garden. There are also many
sophisticated types, such as Catherine
Sharp, Floraine, and John Wallmark,
that belong with that sweet Violet
group listed as *Viola cornuta* and
odorata. They will take off and multiply where conditions suit them, carpet-
ing the woodlands. The variety Royal
Robe is the one which I recommend.

How many know the Golden Star,
a native of our area, belonging to the
Daisy family? It is botanically listed as
Chrysogonum virginianum and grows
eight to ten inches including the perfect
star-shaped flowers that will bloom for
over a month in early spring. It is not a
common plant but worthwhile hunting,
for once established, it will multiply
readily in sun or semi-shade.

Periwinkle in bloom is a thrill,
especially if accentuated with protruding Lilliputian bulbous plants such
as Snowdrops, *Galanthus nivalis,*
Glory of the Snow, *Chionodoxa luci-
liae,* Spring Snowflakes, *Leucojum
vernum,* Grape hyacinths, *Muscari
plumosum album,* in various colors or
Wood hyacinths, *Scilla campanulata.*
The main thing to remember at this

time of the year is that to enjoy these
combinations in early spring we must
plan now for bulb planting time in
November.

Periwinkle, *Vinca minor,* can
now be obtained in several varieties.
Consider Bowles, which has large
foliage and deep blue flowers, or Miss
Jekill's White, which has tiny foliage, is
much more prostrate, and has pure
white flowers. Of course the more
rampant type, *Vinca major,* will soon
take over, as it does in open woodlands.

Spring-flowering perennials
which brave delayed cold spells are not
to be overlooked, and I know of none
finer than the English Wallflowers,
Cheiranthus, which came to us via
England, but were originally native to
the Canary Islands and Mediterranean.

Wallflowers have evergreen foliage and although cultivated as biennials, persist as perennials. Some
varieties will grow less than a foot, like
the Tom-Thumb types, while others
grow to nearly two feet, such as the
Monarchs. They range in color from
white to deep red and also come in
many shades of yellow and lavender.
Temperatures dropping below freezing
do not seem to affect their rugged
temperament.

Closely related to Wallflowers and
true biennials are the more sophisticated and highly fragrant Stocks,
Matthiola. Although I have known
them to stand temperatures to twelve
degrees above zero for short periods, I
only recommend them for warmer
parts of our Zone (Zone 8-B), or in
protected gardens. Grown out of doors,
they perform best when supported by
small stakes as their heavy flower
heads may topple them over.

March and early spring offer truly

four-dimensional gardens, and we can select from flowering trees, shrubs, perennials, and ground covers. From these four we can tax our imagination and create spectacular spring effects. It is the season when a wide selection of deciduous Magnolias begins to bloom. The earliest is Dr. Merrill, *Magnolia stellata,* which has a most fragrant white flower. Then *Magnolia soulangeana,* erroneously called the Tulip Magnolia, bursts open its lovely pink saucers. The latest to bloom in that group is *Magnolia soulangeana nigra* with long purple blossoms. This trio will cover the entire month's span.

Among other spectacular performers in the early spring landscape is the Bradford pear, *Pyrus calleryana.* Before its foliage emerges its entire structure becomes enveloped with a mass of small white flower clusters which are foamy with a slight yellow-

Magnolia soulengeana nigra.

ish cast. It grows to twenty-five feet in a fastigiated, pyramidal shape, thus serving as a perfect accent tree. It might well flank a building or form an alley. It has three distinct stages: in bloom, in leaf—glossy with wavy edges and fluttering in the slightest breeze, and in its bronzy tones of autumn.

The Bradford Pear is only a Pear in name, for its fruit matures to less than Pea size. It came here from the Orient for the experimental purpose of being used as an understock, in an effort to defeat the fire blight disease that was rampant among the large-fruited Pears. In this manner it would serve only as a disease resistant root-stock, with the desired variety being grafted or budded onto it.

It eventually came under the scrutiny of Dr. John Creech, then plant explorer for the United States Department of Agriculture Plant Research Station at Beltsville, Maryland, in the late fifties. From among the many seedlings, one plant stood out in form and autumn coloration. It was grafted on to other seedlings and released to commerce as an ornamental under the name of the Bradford Pear, to honor Dr. Bradford, the director of the station at the time. As such it has become one of the most used and valuable ornamentals, exemplifing the way many plants travel twisted trails of fortuitous migration. Somehow we seem to appreciate them more when we know their origins.

Flowering Cherries, Plums, and Peaches vie for our attention at this time of the year. One of the Cherries, *Prunus subhirtella autumnalis,* is particularly attractive to me because it blooms in early spring and repeats again in late autumn. It can be accel-

Bradford Pear, *Pyrus calleryana*.

erated by the weather.

It is a most graceful small tree growing to twelve feet, which, in bloom, has pendulous branches loaded with Almond-scented, semi-double flowers in delicate pink. It could be grown as a tall shrub or in any manner you choose to trim it. Of course, the sturdier tree-type varieties, Akebono and Kwanzan, made famous in Washington, D. C., as a gift from Japan, are likewise most desirable.

Flowering Crabs, *Malus,* offer a tremendous selection, attracting attention both in flower and later in their fruiting stage. Consider for instance the variety Red Jade, whose tiny fruit appears in autumn as large red berries along the naked stems of pendulous branches. This is one to scrutinize for limited garden space. Another, Dolgo, is one of the first to open its large, pure white blossoms in the spring, followed by extra-large crimson fruit that ripens around August and is most desirable for jelly-making.

Red Jade, *Malus,* in fruit.

The Flowering Plums belong in the same family. Some commonly known as purple-leaved Plums are primarily grown for their attractive summer foliage. The Flowering Plum is one of the most select and stands out in the summer landscape.

This group of early-flowering trees, some of which can be used as small shade trees, are an important part of the spring quartet. The fourth group which completes the seasonal display are the flowering shrubs which greet us with an abundance of blooms.

Although many spring shrubs are well known to us, we often do not realize the assorted varieties from which we can choose. Among the *Forsythia,* for example, Lynwood Gold, a newer one, grows erect to over five feet with flowers all along its stem. Most prolific, this variety responds best to being cut back to one foot above the ground each year after flowering, as it will reproduce its new cane within the year. The weeping *Forsythia suspensa,* a contrasting form, should be planted where it will drape itself over a wall or bank. Just remove some of the older canes each year and they will be replaced by others, with the same lovely weeping growth habit.

Spring Glory is another variety with pale yellow flowers and intermediary growth. There are also dwarf varieties such as Arnold's Dwarf, which grows less than three feet in six years, but will be seven feet across. Thank you, Mother Asia, for giving us such a wonderful plant, and England, for developing most of the modern ones.

Unquestionably one of the better known shrubs, formerly known as Japanese Quince or *Cydonia,* but now reclassified as *Chaenomeles,* fills a crucial place in our gardens. It has value if for no other reason than for its naked stems which can be cut and forced into flower anytime after the New Year. In fact, during years when unusual spring-like weather occurs prematurely it will flower on its own, braving the subsequent cold spells that may occur.

It is thorny and forms an excellent barrier hedge, especially Spitfire, an upright grower to six or seven feet tall in maturity, but seldom over two feet broad. It is well-named as its blossom is bright red and it produces large crimson fruit which is excellent for jelly-making. Another variety, Knap-hill, only grows half that tall and is likewise useful for low hedges in the same color range.

Nivalis is the best of the pure white flowering varieties, producing long stems for cutting. Cameo is apricot and Phillis Moore a lovely pink. No garden can afford to be without these jewels of the Orient, which seem to thrive under almost any treatment. They flower best in full sun, but will tolerate up to half-shade.

For the shady garden, who can resist the *Pieris japonica,* whose white clusters of Lily-of-the-Valley-like flowers dance gracefully in the March winds. There are many species of these often sold as Andromeda. The American species, *Pieris floribunda,* is a native of our southeastern states, but cannot rival its Japanese cousin, which grows to ten feet if permitted the space to expand.

The foliage of Andromeda, which is persistent and evergreen, will not retain its glossiness when planted in the full sun or against buildings that may reflect heat. Truly a woodland

Flowering Quince, *Chaenomeles laglendria contorta.* National Arboretum photo.

plant that thrives in peaty soil, it will take the spotlight while in bloom for a month or more, especially if surrounded with some early spring bulbs. The seed-pods that follow and the bronzy tone of its foliage in the fall cause it to be acclaimed as one of the best nature can offer.

Culminating the flora of March is the Camellia. This genus, which has performed so well throughout the inclement months of winter, reaches its apex as the less hardy plants commence their spring blooming schedule. Refer to the Camellia chapter for plants that flower in March, and be sure to attend the shows to keep abreast of the newer varieties.

March Work Schedule

It could be truly said that March is prevention month, as many of the ills that befall plants can now be eradicated at their source. Over the winter many insects have hybernated and will soon breed along the stems of plants, in the previous year's litter, under the bark of old trees and shrubs, and wherever shrubs have accumulated an overabundance of growth.

The main reason commercial orchardists prune their trees of unwanted and superfluous growth, resulting in an open vase-shaped superstructure, is to allow the sunlight and air to penetrate from above; this not only discourages disease but encourages better fruit formation. They also use a special tool to remove accumulated scaly bark which is especially prevalent on Apple trees. After the debris is destroyed and before the flower buds appear, a dormant spray is applied under high pressure. This process is good common sense, and should be done by the home gardener, even for a single tree.

Dormant sprays, which come under many labels and formulas, have become a cure-all for many plant ills, although I hasten to say that all do not need it. In fact it is my belief that much harm can result when spray is applied indiscriminately under the guise of preventative spraying as practiced by many who use it as a source of revenue and are not licensed or trained in its use.

The best advice I can give is to remind you that nature has provided many checks and balances in the form of parasites to certain insects, and counter-spores to certain diseases; besides, science supplies us with plants bred to resist certain diseases, such as wilt-resisting Tomato varieties. All of these become important tools in our quest for clean and beautiful gardens.

It therefore remains for me to anticipate from month to month those ills which are most prevalent in Zone 8 and could or should be controlled with a spray. Because the control of insects and diseases is most complex, with the remedies changing from year to year, we are fortunate the United States Department of Agriculture, with its vast reservoir of research and information to which are harnessed nationwide research stations and county agents, remains at our service. With the free informative bulletins that are available, we have no excuse for unclean gardens.

The bulletins will point out that certain fruit trees need an unusual type of dormant spray, while others, like Fig trees and Persimmons, need no spray at all. You will also find that to keep that worm from getting into the Apple, a follow-up spray is necessary. Proper equipment, in keeping with the size of the operation and best suited to the problem, is imperative. All of this information is free, which many home gardeners do not realize. Dealing with a garden center or supply house with a good local reputation is another good line of defense.

Another important point in the control of insects is the realization that insects have taste buds sensitive to such an extent that they will devour the foliage of one variety of plant without touching another of the same species. A case in point is that of the most volatile white fly, whose egg masses overwinter on the foliage of certain evergreens such as *Azalea indica alba,* hatching in early spring to feed on its parent plant, yet not touching Kurume varieties of Azaleas. Therefore, saturating an entire planting with a spray program is not only wasteful, but tends to lessen the vigor of those which do not need it.

In seeking to combat the abuse of insecticides, science has made great strides, even to the extent of outlawing certain miracle chemicals of a few years ago such as DDT and Dieldren.

Those that I might recommend are too numerous to mention, some too complicated for the average home gardener to handle. Because of the constantly changing use of insecticides the best advice I can give you is to consult your local experts; many of the best things in life are free.

We might also mention at this time the importance of starting the growing year with good sanitation. All of last year's debris, where many insects and spore diseases over-wintered, should be removed and placed in a compost heap, where it will be neutralized through a process of self-sterilization by bacterial action and concentrated heat. There are commercial ingredients available to accelerate the process if desired.

There are many compost grinders on the market now that play an important role in gardening. Although these machines seem expensive initially, they more than pay for themselves in the long run. Taking up little space, a grinder will spew out rich material to be used as mulch or composted for use as nature's best soil enrichment. I rarely recommend expensive gadgetry, but I have found a compost grinder to be a sound investment. Self-contained compost makers are also on the market for those who wish to have instant compost.

Sanitation is a must, and it should not only start in March, but continue during the entire growing cycle of any plant, from the picking of a Rose leaf showing black spot spores, to the invigorating practice of keeping spent flowers away from annuals and other continuous-blooming plants. Few realize that this simple pruning process prevents plants from setting seeds and halts their dormancy period, prolonging their productivity.

A good gardener has two major trademarks, the possession of the best pruning shears that money can buy in one back pocket and a good sharp knife in another; these two are the most essential tools for sanitary gardening, as well as for shaping the destiny and character of the garden. For as Aristotle said, "Nature has the will, but not the power, to reach perfection."

Good pruning knife.

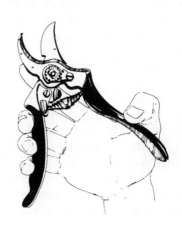

Good shears with two cutting edges.

This month we are particularly reminded that as shrubs complete their flowering sequence they are ready through nature's own dictate and evolution to renew themselves for another season's go-around. Much of the new growth will be superfluous and overpowering. Although older limbs will die out, good gardeners must intervene for the plant to achieve its potential splendor. This is why I say to you that the pruning shear is one of the main tools necessary to keep your dream garden in a state of continuing perfection.

This pruning business starts right now, when the early Forsythia goes out of bloom along with other early flowering shrubs and ornamental trees. Other plants will need attention over the entire year, and there is a good rule of thumb governing this process. Plants that flower after mid-year can be pruned during early spring, as their flowering branches will be formed on the current year's growth, while spring-blooming shrubs and trees are in their formative stage after mid-year, and must not be pruned until after their flowering sequence.

One variance to this rule applies to shrubs whose main feature is berried stems. In their case we must wait not only until after they have flowered, but also until their fruit is set, generally in April. Then they should be nipped off, removing only their new growth, which will intensify their berried clusters. Heavy pruning to rejuvenate an old plant or reduce its size should also be accomplished at this time. Among the shrubs requiring such treatment are Hollies, Pyracanthas, Cotoneasters, and Nandinas. Most of these are equally as beautiful in flower as they are in fruit.

Lawns are an important phase of spring work in the garden, and a must during March is the application of pre-emergent crab grass control, which should be done before this pesty weed germinates. This scientifically formulated chemical halts its germination and is far simpler than the techniques necessary to eradicate it later on. Be sure to have some on hand and apply the right quantity at the right time, according to the instructions on your material. Some fertilizer manufacturers include pre-emergents in their mixtures.

This brings about the question of how much fertilizer should be applied to lawns, covered in more detail under general lawn care. May I say now that fertilizer as applied to any plant cannot be generalized and will be found under specific plant instructions under special chapters. I can warn you, however, that over my long experience and observation of the application of fertilizer, the ills of plants are seldom cured through its agency, unless the lack of its content has been predetermined.

A plant pathologist, for instance, may interpret the need of iron sulfate for your Azaleas by its prominent veining and lack of chlorophyll in the foliage, but this can also be caused by an infestation of spider mites. You can learn these things and interpret them as you gain experience. But never be misled by the idea that fertilizer is a cure-all, as we are often asked to believe by unscrupulous advertisers.

March is not only one of our best planting months, but also one during which we can move things about, or incorporate ground covers in our landscape. It upsets me to see new plantings, such as trees and shrubs, grown over with grass and weeds when so many fine ground covers are available to use as mulch, doing equally well in shade or sun. Besides incorporating another dimension in the landscape they can act as a buffer zone, preventing the barking of young tender trees, and by eliminating all hand-trimming make the mowing of grass a breeze.

Change is the theme of March, and this is the month best suited for the grafting of Camellias, fully explained in the Camellia chapter. What a thrill to be able to change over an old and inferior variety to another, a real Dr. Jekyll and Mr. Hyde act.

Other plant groups discussed in specific chapters which demand a great deal of attention in March are Roses and Vegetables.

Yes, spring invades Zone 8 with a vengeance in March. The entire year's enjoyment of our garden depends on what we accomplish in this month, one of the busiest in a gardener's calendar.

April

Because seasonal changes and natural phenomena are perhaps more influential during April than any other month, we approach it with a greater thrill. The lunar system predicates that Easter is early some years and later others. I cannot explain these mysteries, but if you had gardened through as many Paschal moons as I have, you would have great respect for its influence on the chemistry of plants.

Perhaps no other time of the year can we appreciate the overwhelming evidence of nature's bounty, coming to us from the four corners of the earth. It is a good time to meditate, and express thanksgiving not only to nature, but to those who, often at the risk of their lives, have pursued the rare and beautiful plants of the world, providing us with a varied and colorful world of flora.

May I walk you through my own humble garden that has taken me over thirty years to assemble and which over those years has changed tenants many times, some leaving on their own free will, as they no doubt didn't like the way I treated them, but others evicted, for as time marches on I continually search for the best.

Part of my three acres is native, with Loblolly Pines and Oaks and other hardwoods, upon which climbed a goodly amount of Carolina Yellow Jessamine, *Gelsemium sempervirens,* an evergreen vine at its peak at this season. Nearby a Shadbush bursts into bloom, foretelling the "running of the shad" according to old wives' tales from whence it gets its name. This shrub, which sometimes grows into a small tree of twenty feet or so, has unpredictable flowering habits, sometimes blooming in March to confound gardeners and fishermen alike. The flower is followed in May by a berry of such delicious quality that the more competetive birds almost always devour them on sight, depriving our human appetites. Perhaps this is an explanation of another common name by which it is sold, the Service Berry.

The wooded part of my garden is bordered by marshy waters, and I have kept it very much the way nature gave it to me. My main additions have been Camellias, always my favorite in the plant world, and Azaleas, so at home in a woodland setting although they explode into brilliant colors every spring. Rhododendrons also prosper here and make good companions for the other plants. A few Clerodendrons volunteered to provide me with summer color, and I have planted Hydrangeas to dot the warmer days with their cooling shades of blue.

I plant only what I love in the woods, and I have always been drawn to their shade and comfort for quiet contemplation. A gnarled and broken Cedar Tree has overturned to provide me with a perfect vantage point to watch the water birds and marsh life which seem to enjoy the spot as much as I. And to prove the resiliency of nature, although the Cedar lies fallen, it starts new growth several feet up the embankment.

In the more formal part of my garden, the Hackberry Tree, which I describe in December, is leafing now, and the *Mondo* grass has been pruned down to the ground. The flowering Quince is blooming and the Mock Orange and Viburnum bring excitement to this area. It won't be long before the Cardinal Flower will appear on the border of my terrace, and I always look forward to the summer blooming of the *Gordonia lasianthus.*

To the side of my home an arched trellis is already in bloom with Clematis and the perennial Peonies are in close pursuit of the now fading Tree Peonies. Staked to form graceful trees, the American Honeysuckle is flowering and will do so until frost.

There is no time when my garden is without a blooming plant. This summer when many yards are bare save for the grass and a few annuals, my front area will be full of color for passers-by to enjoy. The Peonies which border the street area will be gone, but the Roses, both hybrid and shrub varieties, will

flower until fall. Joining them will be the seldom-grown Hypericum, which produces bright yellow Buttercup-like flowers all summer. Soon the Achillea and Rose Mallow will bloom and the unusual white Althea Diane, which borders my neighbor's property, will make a flowering hedge.

There are many other occupants throughout my yard. A Holly garden gives me winter pleasure, and of course, the Anise Tree and Strawberry Bush are two of my favorites. I have always enjoyed trying plants from other regions, and am pleased to see a ten year old Pistachio Tree which I got from California in fruit for the first time.

I won't list every plant I've chosen for my garden, but encourage you to seek out the unusual and you, too, may be rewarded not only with a favorite plant but a conversation piece for your visitors.

The bicentennial year broke many gardening records this month in our portion of the temperate zone. The native Dogwood, *Cornus florida,* for instance, was at its peak the first week of April, at least two weeks ahead of normal, but before the month ended the time schedule re-adjusted itself and the majority of the plant world behaved quite normally. So, regardless of what tricks nature plays, never reset your garden clock, but keep your eye on the averages, which are always part of your weather report.

Unquestionably the Dogwoods, because they are part of our native flora, have become a permanent part of our American gardens wherever they can be cultivated. And I can well remember when the first pink clone was discovered. Now these soft pastels

Dogwood, *Cornus florida.*

flowers found on Cherokee Princess and others. Cloud 9 is one such variety that is not only more prolific but blooms much earlier than Cherokee Chief.

An important point to remember in planting Dogwoods is that these new and patented varieties are budded plants, meaning that their root systems are still native. Although nursery-grown specimens transplant with fair success, there are more Dogwood seedlings taken from the wild that never make it, than those that do. The main reason for failure is that they normally have more roots than top; a three foot plant will often have five feet of root system tangled in with other native roots. Many years ago a wise old gardener told me how to overcome this.

have been hybridized to deep pinks and nearly-reds, the deepest shades belonging to Cherokee Chief. Always purchase Dogwoods in bloom, for you may find that you prefer the larger but paler

Pick out a Dogwood whose trunk diameter is less than a broom handle,

in March cut wild seedling and plant

after plant sprouts in June or July, cut back, leaving strongest shoot

Cutting and planting wild Dogwood.

36

early in the spring, before the foliage forms; dig it up bare-rooted with as many roots as you can salvage; cut all the straggling roots back to a foot and plant it in good woodsy soil. Water it immediately and cut the top down to less than a foot above the ground. Wait for about a month, and soon several shoots will emerge from near the root portion. Let these grow for the rest of the summer and then pick out the strongest leader. Eliminate all the others and remove the original stump with a sharp saw or lopping shear.

Within two years that particular shoot will have reached in height and diameter the size plant with which you started. This method of handling Dogwoods from the wild is sound and can be used for many other plants. The simple reason is that wild seedlings shifting for themselves do not form a ball-like root structure like the ones rooted and grown in nurseries. Remember this when you are tempted to pull up wild seedlings and cram them in the trunk of a car or expose them to the whipping of the wind, with each minute drying out the precious moisture from the stems and roots.

About the time our Dogwood is in bloom, the native Redbud, *Cercis canadensis,* appears on the scene, and the two often vie for attention in their natural habitat along the edge of woodlands. Its common name comes from its buds, which first emerge with a reddish caste before opening with pinkish-lavender flowers. It has been replaced in commerce with the Chinese species, *Cercis chinensis,* which normally blooms a little later with a deeper rosy-purple flower. Both grow to forty feet if permitted, but can be held to ten to fifteen foot shrubs through yearly

pruning after they have finished blooming.

The comparison of these two species brings into focus how fortunate we are to be able to garnish our gardens with both native and exotic plants. For instance, this is the month Azaleas dot our landscape, and while we have many beautiful native species, most of which are deciduous, the Oriental evergreen species have supplanted ours, especially in the areas covered by this book.

From Virginia south through the Carolinas to Florida, many native species, generally known as swamp Azaleas, thrive along the lowlands. In Virginia and southward we have the Pinxterbloom, *A. nudiflorum,* the coast Azalea, *A. atlanticum,* and others, mostly sweet-scented and beautifully at home in the wild garden. They cannot vie, however, with the vivid colors of the Oriental species which have invaded the southeast. I have prepared a chapter on Azaleas to guide you in the selection of those that will not only fit the small garden, but can be in bloom from late March through late May.

Azaleas are closely related to Rhododendrons; in fact modern books classify both as Rhododendrons. I have elected to keep the two separate for simplification. As Rhododendrons normally follow Azaleas in their blooming sequence, I will tell you about them under the May time table. We have many native species whose habitats are in the higher elevations covered in our zone, but with careful handling and selective emplacement will thrive within the tidal lowlands. In short, whereas these beautiful Rhododendrons bloom naturally along the open ridges of our Appalachian range, many will do beautifully under the protection and filtered sunlight of trees nearer the coast, as do our Azaleas.

The Chinese Photinia, *P. serrulata,* was introduced to western gardens around 1800 and has proven an ideal evergreen shrub, growing to twenty-five feet. A newer hybrid, *P. fraserii,* is a little more hardy and like the former blooms at this time of the year with large umbels of white flowers. However, this is only part of their quality, for in late summer and early fall clusters of brilliant small berries emerge that persist until devoured by the birds.

Unfortunately, Photinias are often offered by the trade as small evergreen plants and used as hedges, or planted where they do not have the opportunity to expand as large specimen shrubs nor perform throughout the entire year in all of their seasonal splendor. Their lustrous foliage of green leaves to eight inches long turns a deep autumn shade of nearly fiery red, and in combination with the berried clusters, is something to behold. Then in early spring, prior to their blooming sequence, new unfurling foliage cloaks the shrub in auburn tones before resuming their greener summer hues. Few plants in our landscape can compete with Photinia's versatility if given a place in the sun. These are not to be confused with *Photinia villosa,* a most worthy deciduous shrub of more upright growth, which grows much farther north than the evergreen types, which are generally hardy only to the Washington, D.C., area and south.

April ushers in many of the Viburnums, a most diversified group of shrubs, with species grown for both their flowers and fruit. Gathered from all over the world, including our own continent, they are often referred to as Snowballs by novices. This can be misleading, for not all of their flowers are shaped like snowballs; some resemble wild Carrots or Queen Anne's Lace.

In the selection of Viburnums one may choose between the native varieties that are largely known for their fruiting clusters which appear in late summer, or the Orientals that are better known for their flowers. Three of the best in the fruiting category are the Linden Viburnum, *V. dilatatum,* the

Once a small gift to my neighbor, this *Photinia serrulata* now dwarfs me.

Tea Viburnum, *V. theiferum,* and the Wrights variety, *V. wrighti.* Although showier in the fall, even these species have an April blossom.

However, for fragrance and sheer beauty in early April, few Viburnum can vie with the fragrant Snowball, *V. carlcephalum,* which was hybridized in England and is a progeny of the Spice Viburnum, *V. carlesi,* a Korean species with smaller snowball-like flowers.

Viburnum carlcephalum. National Arboretum photo.

This has become my favorite after growing dozens of other types.

On the other hand, many favor the Mariesi variety of the *Viburnum tomentosum*, which is notable for its two season performance. Some even claim that it rivals the Dogwood in both the spring with its snowball blossoms and again in the fall when its autumn foliage is studded with brilliant red berries. This is not to be confused with the true Japanese Snowball, *V. tomentosum plicatum*, which blooms a month later and does not bear berries. All of these mentioned are deciduous and must be seen to be appreciated.

There are also a few evergreens worthy of mention. A favorite of southern gardens is *V. laurestinus,* or *V. tinus,* a native of the Mediterranean region and quite tender and apt to winter kill in the colder portions of our zone. And yet, under the coldest conditions it will often sucker back and grow to ten feet tall. Its performance is most amazing because of its ability to flower throughout late winter and early spring in clusters of the most fragrant white to pinkish flowers, which are normally followed with metallic blue berries, turning black. Like all Viburnums, it prefers full sun but will tolerate some shade. Because it has small foliage, which averages an inch long, and a flexible limb structure, it is often used as an evergreen hedge, or espaliered against a southern exposed wall.

The sweet evergreen Viburnum, *V. odoratissimum,* a native of India and Japan, looks more like a Laurel and grows to fifteen feet with large glossy foliage six or more inches long and is useful as a tall hedge or screen. It has a habit of spreading itself through underground runners and will soon take over if unrestricted. It too may be on the tender side, but is excellent to shield out objectionable features in the landscape. Another variety similar in growing habit is the Leatherleaf Viburnum, *V. rhytidophyllum,* from western China. It is very hardy, and although it blooms at this time of the year it is most effective in the fall when its red and black berries contrast so vividly against its rugged foliage.

The list of Viburnums goes on and on. There is no doubt that it is one of our most versatile shrubs and should be included in every yard.

Nearly as numerous are the Cotoneasters, a family of plants primarily originating in the cooler regions of northern Asia, which in part explains why some of them succumb to the so-called fire blight disease in our zone. I will just mention a few, some evergreen, others deciduous, which I believe are worthwhile cultivating. The deciduous types, *C. divaricata* and *C. dielsiana,* are the most resistant to disease and are exceptionally good as five to six foot shrubs. They also make graceful hedges, flowering at this time with small pink flowers which later produce scarlet berries, in contrast to their autumn foliage. There is a dwarf form, *C. apiculata,* known as the Cranberry Cotoneaster, which grows to only two feet.

My favorite among the evergreen types is *Cotoneaster lactea,* which grows to eight feet. Unfortunately it is rare in the American trade, but worth having your favorite nursery or garden center order for you since it is equally beautiful in flower as when berry-laden. The low prostrate types such as *Cotoneaster horizontalis,* are beautiful, but best suited to the cooler regions, where the fire blight disease is not as rampant.

Speaking of the cooler regions reminds us that Lilacs, *Syringa,* are not happy in most of our zone, although they will tolerate it if given ideal conditions under which to grow. First provide them with an alkaline soil, a continuous supply of lime, their favorite fertilizer, bonemeal, and a relatively well-drained soil. Under such auspices, I have seen good Lilacs grow. And, of course, every one loves them at this time of the year. They should be severely pruned after flowering to encourage a constant supply of new growth because the older canes attract borers and scale. Some of the Chinese and Korean species, *S. microphylla* and *S. palibiniana,* are tolerant of our climate and also possess a marvelously elusive fragrance.

Other more hardy invaders from the north are the Spiraeas, of which there are over a hundred species known to commerce. Most every one knows the Bridal Wreath, although several species are often confused under this common name. One is *S. thunbergi,*

Spiraea

which is possibly the earliest to bloom, sometimes flowering in the winter before the arrival of spring, and another is *Spiraea vanhouttei.* Both grow to over six feet tall with a weeping habit.

One of the most dwarf of the Spiraeas, of recent introduction from England although a native of Japan, is

Spiraea japonica alpina. It grows to less than a foot and is most sought after since the plants make a dense mound of foliage and blooms with flat clusters of small pink flowers. The hybrids of *Spiraea bumalda,* which grow to three feet, likewise produce flat clusters of flowers ranging from pink to red.

The one that most closely resembles the Bridal Wreath form is *Spiraea prunifolia,* one of the earliest introduced from Japan around 1843. It is still found in some of the old gardens and has double white flowers the size of small buttons. It grows to eight or more feet, but like all Spiraea, can be controlled through annual pruning. Some pink sports of these are carried by certain nurseries, and prized by many gardeners.

From among these you will find an easy to cultivate Spiraea that will meet your needs.

Due to their susceptibility to fire blight and other diseases, Hawthorns are not the easiest of shrubs to grow south of the Mason-Dixon line, but the so-called Yeddo-Hawthorn, *Raphiolepis umbellata,* introduced from Japan around 1850, is a beautiful substitute. A charming evergreen, it grows to over six feet, with fragrant blossoms produced in upright panicles. However, it took California nurseries to hybridize them and bring out many named varieties, which are more compact in growth and therefore more adaptable to the home garden. Enchantress with its deep pink blossoms and Pink Cloud are among many available.

Yeddo-Hawthorns will stand full sun or half-shade, and are happy in the same soil condition as Azaleas and Camellias, and therefore are good companion plants. Their foliage colors up in the fall and they produce black berries the size of Peas. Unlike Hawthorns, they are thornless.

Another acid-loving plant for such a setting is *Enkianthus campanulatus,* also an introduction from Japan. Unfortunately, it has no common name, but the plant somewhat resembles a Blueberry bush with the same pendulous small bell-shaped flowers in clusters. They are deciduous and do not produce fruit but are extremely ornamental while in bloom at this time of the year. Pruning will easily keep them smaller than their natural size of six feet or more.

There is always a need for a plant that will grow on impoverished soil, such as Scotch Broom, *Cytisus scoparius,* a nomad from southeastern Europe. The story I like best about Scotch Brooms claims they hitchhiked to America via the fodder for the Hessian cavalry during the Revolutionary War and spread from Yorktown, Virginia. It is said that Thomas Jefferson liked this shrub so well that he always carried seeds in his pocket to give away when he traveled.

While they are not evergreen, the stems are green and the foliage so small that they have the appearance of an evergreen plant. Growing to five feet on willowy stems, they produce Pealike golden blossoms in profusion, and are most spectacular at this time of the year. Dotting the countryside wherever their seeds may fall, they offer a colorful surprise scrambling up the side of a scooped-out gravel pit or dangling along the dry banks of a super highway.

Hybridists have brought out many species of Scotch Broom with different colored blooms ranging to deep pink

Scotch Broom, *Cytisus scoparius,* along Virginia's Route 64.

weeks later.

If you should have a place where intruders need to be repelled, then the Hardy Orange, *Poncirus trifoliata,* will make a perfect deciduous hedge growing to twelve or more feet. At this time of the year it produces white flowers followed by a fruit which gives it its common name. It is most ornamental at all seasons, and its sharp spines will discourage man or beast.

Among the most spectacular of the twining vines in April are the Wisterias. Due to their rampant nature they must be grown and confined to a durable arbor or trellis; otherwise, if left on their own, will soon overpower any given location or tree in the average home's yard. Not only will the vine itself grow three to five feet a year, eventually becoming fifty or more feet, but their avaricious root system will take over the yard. The planting and care of these beautiful vines are of the utmost consideration. I would suggest

that can be purchased from such seed houses as Park's. After the plant is a couple of years old, it is best to cut it down each year after its blooming period. It will then renew itself from the base of the plant, and flower on the current year's growth. If not cut back it will produce a lot of dead tops. Do not use any fertilizer to stimulate it.

Wilson's Pearlbush, *Exochorda wilsoni,* was introduced in America in 1907 and produces a profusion of white flowers two inches in diameter. Although it is a most vigorous deciduous shrub to twelve feet, it has a short duration in flower, and I would rather wait for the *Philadelphus* a couple of

Hardy Orange, *Poncirus trifoliata.* National Arboretum photo.

planting them in a twelve to fourteen inch concrete pipe sunk three feet with the bell joint left above ground. In that manner you will confine the root system from overpowering any other nearby plantings.

Plant Wisterias in ordinary soil without added fertilizer. This also applies to tree types, which are available grafted onto a single trunk-like support. They both require strong restriction through pruning at least twice a year, once during the summer when they are making their strongest growth, and again in the winter while dormant. Cut them back to their flowering buds, which are evident.

There are several types offered, most of which are the Chinese species *Wisteria floribunda chinensis,* sold under many names and colors ranging from white to the deep lavender which is the most fragrant. The length of their flower clusters will range from two to over three feet, and when trained horizontally along some classical high pillared building, as I saw it at Sweet Briar College in Virginia, it is really a sight to behold.

Our native species, *Wisteria frutescens,* is a much better type for the small home since the flower clusters grow to only six inches. The vines are not as rampant and flower over a much longer period, repeating during the late spring and summer months. You can see it planted around Colonial Williamsburg.

Tree Peonies, once cultivated primarily in botanical gardens and large private estates, are now offered commercially at reasonable prices at better garden centers and mail-order houses. This is due to a transition of modern packing, shipping, and growing tech-

Wisteria.

niques. Most of the Tree Peonies are botanically classified as *Paeonia suffruticosa moutan* and should not be confused with the regular and better known herbaceous perennial type which, to avoid confusion, will be recognized here as the perennial Peony.

The difference in the two is that Tree Peonies are actually a shrub growing to five or more feet, while the regular perennial dies back to the ground each year and normally blooms later. Their combination in the garden gives a new dimension to this noble and long lasting genus, which will often span generations. The tree type, while growing under the same soil condition as the other, requires deeper planting by three to four inches than the perennial type, which needs to have its noticeable growth buds near the surface.

Neither likes to be disturbed once planted, so the soil should be well prepared. Perferably you should create a pocket of soil, loosened and dug to at least a foot and covered with an ample layer of well-decayed stable manure. Mix in at least a quart of limestone per square yard of soil, in conjunction with a quart of bonemeal. This square yard preparation will give each plant a reserve resource for expansion. A sprinkling of bonemeal should also be included in the excavated soil to serve as a backfill. Remember that Peonies last for a century, and that as time goes on they will only need a good annual mulch of some sort, along with a top dressing of more well-rotted animal manure, and an occasional sprinkling of bonemeal and lime. Tree Peonies are more expensive than the perennials, but are an investment in the April landscape with results few other plants can match. It pays to buy the best of each from specialists, for their colors and forms are numerous, and they repeat each year with increasing abundance.

The Iris family of perennial plants is most numerous and varied, but the German or tall-bearded species *Iris germanica,* now in bloom, is among the most spectacular. However, we are told by Iris fanciers that the flowers can be had in bloom every month of the year from the dwarf type *I. pumila* to giant flowering Japanese species mentioned in our May parade of plants. For selection of Iris, as well as its individual cultivation and needs, join your local Iris society or avail yourself of the many catalogs and other literature devoted to their selection.

April Work Schedule

There are possibly more plants offered for sale in April than any other month, and therefore more planting is done at this time. However in the general area of Zone 8 the best planting season for hardy shrubs, trees, and vines as well as perennials is from mid-September to January. Our wonderful cool falls and mild winters give plants an invigorating start and long recuperating period. This, of course, will be emphasized under the work schedules for the fall months.

Nevertheless, we are lured by the opportunity to plant things in full bloom, such as Azaleas, Rhododendrons, and many others, even Roses. This is particularly true since the advent of container growing and the packing and shipping facilities which can now offer plants at their most attractive stage, even when out of season for our particular area. And I hasten to say that there is nothing wrong with this practice, if we adhere to certain observations.

First and foremost, plants should be removed from their containers, especially those encased in tin or other non-decaying material. All good reliable garden centers will help you do this by splitting such containers open with a temporary tie for easy removal. This will also give you the opportunity to examine the root system, for if extra-rootbound, the plant's survival may be in jeopardy.

As a result of forced watering and feeding, the root system has survived in a small amount of soil relative to the size of the plant itself. This does not always encourage readjustment to an open ground situation unless great care is given the plant until such time as the roots have had a chance to deploy in a natural fashion. Therefore many casualties occur when transferring a plant from a container, whereas a nursery plant of the same kind purchased in a burlap bag would survive. An explanation on how to best handle a container-grown plant can be found in the October work schedule.

Spring planting of trees, shrubs,

perennials, and others always demands more attention than fall planting, especially when it comes to watering, which occasionally is lacking in a natural form at the time when it is most required. It is also good to remember the old adage that a fifty cent tree in a dollar hole is better than a dollar tree in a fifty cent hole, which of course applies at any time. Spring planting is a common practice, especially when we have voids in the landscape that must be filled. This is the reason it is noted in April, although some planting may start in March, and May 1 is the deadline that I recommend.

With the flush of early spring color waning from the bulbs, we must precipitate a continuum of flowers by planting annuals. It is best to insert seedlings in between the ripening bulb tops, and others can be sown directly from seed. An old method of doing this is to mix the contents of a seed packet with a handful of dry sand and thereby affect a more even distribution.

For your consideration I have selected forty of the easiest annuals to grow, showing the quantity of seed per ounce, which is quite important as an index on how they should be sown. This and information on the planting

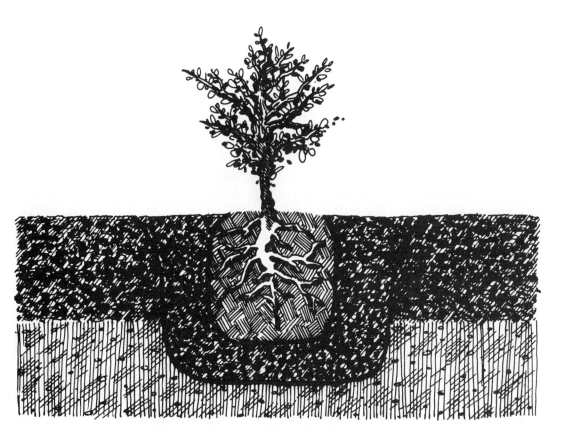

A "dollar hole"—the big investment.

and cultivation of annuals is discussed in the Annuals chapter.

You will also wish to get in a supply of summer-flowering bulbs such as Dahlias, Cannas, and Gladiolas. Incidentally, I have found they over-winter best in place, with a light straw mulch, and should be divided and replanted at this time of the year. Monbretias are another excellent cut flower not as well known as they should be. Caladiums, one of the most showy of the leafy summer annuals, are of course, most tender, and best started in small pots to be planted out in May.

Many home gardeners underestimate the importance of succession in planting with annuals as well as vegetables. For instance, Lettuce can be picked now from early sowings, and must be sown at least monthly for successive harvest using different varieties that will withstand the summer heat.

Be sure to follow through on your pruning schedule as the flowering shrubs complete their blooming period. This is possibly the most important phase of keeping the landscape in balance. Especially examine those shrubs whose berry production will become a major aspect of the fall and winter display, such as Pyracanthas and Hollies. You will note that after the flowers have fallen the berries take their place and, soon thereafter, new stem growth begins. As previously stated in March, this is the time to consider nipping off the elongated growth.

The rule in this case is to let this new growth continue if the plant is still in a juvenile stage until such time that it has reached the desired size. Then this new growth can be stopped by nipping it off beyond the berry cluster. This accomplishes two main purposes, that of keeping the plant within its allocated space and, perhaps most important, concentrating the strength of the plant towards greater berry production for size and intense coloring. This simple factor is often overlooked.

One member of the berried shrubs, the Nandina, has peculiar pruning needs that should also be attended to this month. While nature has provided these plants, when older, with growth buds located behind each leaf-node, the entire leaf never falls off, but leaves a cuticle which dries up and entraps behind it a live bud which also dries up. The pulling down and removal of these cuticles each spring, before growth

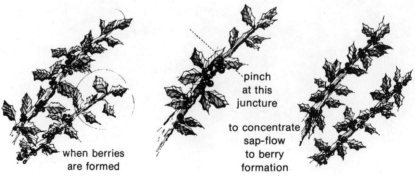

when berries are formed

pinch at this juncture

to concentrate sap-flow to berry formation

Nipping off.

starts, results in bushier Nandinas and lush growth furnished to the ground. This information was given me many years ago by a lady gardener who visited our parks. I was incredulous at the time, but have since experimented with the procedure and can assure you that it works.

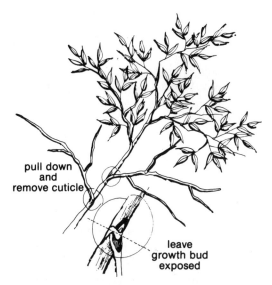

Removing cuticle from Nandina.

May

What better way to introduce May in Zone 8 than through the grand dame of all the flowering broad leaf evergreens, *Magnolia grandiflora.* Somehow I never did like its common name, Bull-Bay, adopted perhaps to impress us with its great strength and resilience during storms. In my experience of observing them through hurricanes their breakage was always minimal, even less than the Live Oak.

As a native to our southern states, it has long been a trademark of the old south's gracious living, and the envy of those areas where it does not thrive. I like to call it the Grand Dame because to be at its best it must have plenty of room to grow and sweep its lower limbs across green avenues of lawn, with its gracefully draped skirts hiding the droppings that otherwise must be picked up at least ten months out of the year.

Unfortunately, as the Magnolia's fragrant white blooms develop and new foliage replaces the old, the leathery old leaves that fall resist the sweeping of any rake ever invented and must be speared one by one to be carted away. Even the compost heap has a hard job disintegrating them, and this process goes on for at least four months. Then the seed capsules also fall to the ground and will stop the most ambitious lawn mower. Well, those of you who have experienced this task know the truth of what I say and have probably lost some of your enchantment with its beauty. But with her skirts to harbor all debris, which eventually turns to humus, the Magnolia never loses her magnificent appeal. That, at least, is the way I like to see it grown.

One clone of *Magnolia grandiflora* called *exoniensis,* advertised some years ago on the west coast, was much slower and more pyramidal in growth, spreading to thirty feet or so. I have not seen it advertised in the last twenty years, which shows again the fickle nature of the nursery business and the necessity for plant lovers to demand more versatility in the commercial market.

Magnolias measure their life spans in centuries, and attain a limb spread of over a hundred feet during their first, a fact to be considered if you intend to confine them to a hundred foot lot. Yet,

I have seen quite a few espaliered, which requires dexterity, patience, and know-how. They thrive from Washington, D. C., south to the Florida border and beyond, and with the Live Oak are among the most outstanding of our native trees.

Another longtime favorite is the Tulip Tree, *Liriodendron tulipifera,* planted at Mount Vernon by George Washington, who valued its shade and flowers. It is so named because its blossoms, which appear at this time of the year, resemble the Tulip in form and size, and are a greenish-yellow color with orange markings. It is a native of our eastern woodland and one of our

The seldom-seen flower of the Tulip Tree, *Liriodendron tulipifera.* National Arboretum photo.

most valuable timber trees, growing over a hundred feet high, with a straight trunk. It is also called Tulip Poplar, which is very confusing because other trees, such as the Tulip Magnolia, are also called Tulip Trees.

This one is deciduous and grows straight up, seldom spreading more than one-quarter its height. Its only trouble is that you seldom see its lovely blooms which locate themselves at the top of the tree in search of light. Because of these characteristics, it is not recommended as a flowering tree, or as a small shade tree.

Another tree with spectacular blooms at this time of the year is the Empress Tree, *Paulownia imperialis,* a nomad from China which has spread itself as far north as New York City, growing under the most impoverished situations, even springing up from the crevices of old foundations. It grows very fast, with tremendous foliage when young, and produces panicles of violet or lilac-colored flowers, followed by interesting seed-pods, which soon spread about in their nomadic search for survival. The limbs are brittle and soon broken up by storms and high winds, which makes the Empress unsatisfactory for areas restricted by space.

Similar to the Empress is the Indian Bean Tree, *Catalpa bignonioides,* also deciduous, which produces large panicles of white flowers. While attractive in bloom and fast growing, I do not recommend it where choice is limited.

The Horse Chestnut or Buckeye Tree, *Aesculus hippocastanum,* a native of America and Europe, is an excellent tree, some types being most spectacular in flower at this time. Our native tree has white blossoms, but

Empress Tree, *Paulownia imperialis*. National Arboretum photo.

there are several hybrid varieties available, such as *A. pavia,* which are red and make up into a small round-headed tree of from fifteen to twenty-five feet high and broad. This tree has made some of the streets of Paris famous in the spring and is worthy of your investigation.

The Virginia Fringetree, *Chionanthus virginicus,* is perhaps one of our most spectacular native deciduous trees along the eastern seaboard, found from New Jersey south to Florida, with six inch long loose white panicles of flowers at this time of the year. In the fall it produces dark blue grape-like clusters of fruit, with its foliage turning a bright yellow. It attains twenty or more feet in stature if given open sunlight and good rich soil.

While not often offered in commerce, it is well worth a search as it is one of those small trees whose performance will lend dignity to its setting. With a ground cover of Lily-of-the-Valley, *Convallaria majalis,* or *Oxalis,* which blooms about the same time,

you can create an unusual Maytime setting for your garden, the kind everyone will remember.

Perhaps one of the most typical shrubs used, or should I say abused, in Zone 8, is the glossy-leaved Privet, a large evergreen which will attain twenty to twenty-five feet in height and breadth in that number of years. It is known and sold in the trade as *Ligustrum lucidum* and normally used as a hedge plant. However, under this form of cultivation it will never develop its full beauty; grown as an individual shrub it will be resplendent at this time of year. The white panicles of flowers, which resemble but are not as fragrant as Lilacs, are followed by black, grape-like clusters of berries, equally as attractive.

If you insist on a Ligustrum hedge, you might try *L. lucidum coriaceum,* which is a dwarf form and will need very little trimming. While its cost may be double, think of the expense in keeping the regular variety to size, a process involving at least six clippings a year. Both have their place in the landscape.

Another large evergreen shrub often misused in the home landscape is

An avenue of tree-size Ligustrum.

the Firethorn, *Pyracantha,* whose many species are, for the most part, from the Orient. This magnificent flowering and berried shrub can be used for tall hedges of eight or more feet, or as solitary specimens growing twenty feet in the full sun. Sometimes they are used with great effect espaliered against a southern wall or high fence, exemplifying once again that plants have many specific uses in the landscape. As there are plenty of all sizes to go around and accomplish any purpose we have in mind, we should always be mindful of each plant's true potential and use it where it can be most enjoyed.

Pittosporum, Tobira, is a glossy-leafed evergreen shrub that blooms at this time of the year with small, fragrant, yellowish tinted flowers. They are followed in the fall by brown seed pods much valued in Christmas arrangements. Although Pittosporum can be grown equally effectively as a specimen or used as a hedge, I have always preferred them pruned as small trees with a single trunk, the way I remember seeing them in the southern part of my native country, France.

May normally brings forth many of the finer deciduous shrubs, of which the Mock Orange, *Philadelphus,* is one of the best. It is one of those shrubs, however, that leaves much to be desired ten months out of the year, as neither its foliage, seedpods, or even its form has any particular charm. But to have it in bloom for a couple of weeks and inhale its delightful fragrance in the landscape is incomparable. If I were limited to one variety among the hundreds offered in commerce, I would select Enchantment, a double-flowering variety with the most elusive fragrance, made famous by Lemoines Nursery in France.

The Pomegranate, *Punica granatum,* introduced here by the early colonists in the deep south, is a native of southeastern Europe. Truly a magnificent deciduous shrub, it grows to twelve feet with deep scarlet flowers an inch or more in diameter, followed by fruit whose coloring defies description as it varies from deep yellow to red. It was named by Pliny, who recommended its various attributes including its fruit for consumption, its bark for tanning, its roots for certain medicinal properties as a vermifuge, and its dried rind for diarrhea and dysentery.

Punica multiflora nana, a dwarf clone of the Pomegranate, grows to eighteen to twenty-four inches and is most attractive. It can be grown from seed to prevail as a perennial, or come inside as a lovely house plant. Everything about it is miniature, flower and fruit. We are indeed fortunate to be able to grow this plant, which is not hardy beyond our zone, but will grow here under most conditions. Its foliage alone is most attractive.

Deutzia is another deciduous shrub made famous by the Lemoines Nursery of France, and while there are many offered in commerce the so-called slender *Deutzia,* Gracilis, is perhaps the best. It grows to three feet and features an avalanche of white flowers in early May. Its foliage is most appealing, especially when the shrub is used as a low hedge.

Other deciduous shrubs that enliven the landscape are *Weigela* and *Kolkwitzia,* both from China, which grow to ten feet with arching branches bearing tubular pink to red flowers for most of the month.

Deutzia crenata. National Arboretum photo.

One of this country's greatest gifts to the world's flora is our Mountain Laurel, *Kalmia latifolia,* seen growing in abundance along our seacoast and mountainous areas. It is at home in the shade, yet will tolerate the full open sun. According to our own whims this evergreen shrub can be maintained as a low hedge or plant through annual pruning, or be allowed to grow to twelve or more feet. It attains its full glory at this time, with its clusters of white to deep pink flowers. Its peculiarly shaped flowers were called Calico Flowers among the early American settlers. It prefers an acid soil, will not tolerate lime in any form, and grows best in woodsy soil, to which it is native, making it a true companion plant to Rhododendrons, Azaleas, and Camellias.

The genus Rhododendron, which includes Azaleas, comprises more species than any other group of ornamental woody plants, with over two thousand listed. Originating from all over the world, many have been cultivated for centuries. Rhododendrons and Azaleas are both native to our Appalachian Mountains, but the Rhododendron's foliage is larger and more heavily textured than the Azalea's and the flowers form in large spherical clusters.

Most Rhododendrons will bloom after the mid-season varieties of Azaleas are through, and are considered an excellent companion plant; their cultivation is much the same, in so far as environment and soil requirements are concerned. Naturally, their space requirement is greater than Azaleas, and they will normally attain ten feet both in height and width. They are generally considered hybrids and their cost is normally double that of Azaleas, which makes them best used as specimen plants in the landscape.

Rhododendrons are becoming more popular and their availability greater since container techniques of growing and shipping them have taken over the nursery industry, permitting the transportation of large quantities of plants over great distances. For some reason the Pacific northwest, a great producer of hybrid Rhododendrons, has monopolized this transition, often creating higher consumer costs.

Rhododendrons are grown in light soil mixtures and under-size containers to avoid greater shipping cost while

Rhododendron. National Arboretum photo.

their full vigor of growth and florescence is maintained through hydroponic stimulants. Therefore, when the plant is left on its own in open culture, even under the best of care, its percentage of survival is minimal. While some plants could survive this, Rhododendrons probably will not, even under a year's guarantee. Therefore it is best to buy the more expensive field-grown plants, which are balled and burlapped and acclimated to our southeastern conditions. And remember, when allowed adequate space in the landscape, Rhododendrons will increase in beauty from year to year.

Among the hundreds of varieties available, I would recommend the following six for the beginner: Pink Pearl, the most sensational of the pink; Cunningham's white; Blue Peter; English Roseum; America, a dark red; and Purpureum Elegans. These will take in the main color range and cover over a month's blooming period. All can be planted in full bloom and should be given ten feet of space, preferably under filtered sunlight as afforded by Pines.

At least a square yard of well decomposed compost, leafmold, or peat moss six inches deep should be dug into the top twelve inches of top soil and a mulch of Pine needles or Pine chips maintained all year. Keep your plant well watered for the first year, and thereafter throughout droughts. This, in short, is your insurance for success with Rhododendrons, which become nigh indestructable if given this start. Taken out of a tin can with tight-bound roots, artificially kept alive in transit, a Rhododendron's chances for survival are one in a hundred unless you are an expert.

In February we enjoyed the fragrance of Daphne odora, which surpasses that of any other shrub. Now one of its relatives, Daphne cneorum, which is deciduous, comes into the picture. It, too, is dwarf, and with its lovely pink flowers has a fragrance similar to the February bloomer. The variety Somerset is one of its most hardy hybrids and will stand light shade. The Daphnes are really a choice lot of Dwarf shrubs, of which another species, D. genkwa, is one of the finest. It blooms ahead of D. cneorum and is a most brillant blue, something quite scarce in the plant world. This one was introduced from Korea in 1843 and needs to be better known.

The herbaceous Peony, Paeonia, so well known to most of us, is really the spectacular of the month of May, and with judicious selection from among the hundreds of varieties offered on the market, can be had in bloom the entire month. We sometimes forget that flowering schedules, as well as color and forms, are necessary to note for successful gardens. It pays to order Peonies from specialists who can advise you on their choice since the original cost is minimal when you figure that each plant becomes an investment in a lifetime of beauty.

Another good investment for the perennial garden is the Gerbera, one of those southern African plants which will tolerate most of Zone 8 winters, especially if grown under a good mulch protection in the full open sun with well drained conditions. Starting to bloom at this time, the Transvaal Daisy, as it is often called, will continue until cut down by frost. Obtainable as plants from specialists, they can also be grown from seeds sown at this time of

My herbaceous Peonies, *Paeonia*, delight me every spring.

the year to flower the next. The same method applies to another South African plant, commonly called Red-Hot-Poker-Plant or *Tritoma*. Now add Snapdragons, *Anthirrhinums*, Foxglove, *Digitalis* and Columbines, *Aquilegia*, and your perennial border will come alive at this time of the year.

One of the lesser known perennials blooming at this time of the year is the hardy Gloxinia, *Incarvillea delavayi*, so called because its blossoms resemble that exotic greenhouse plant the Gloxinia. Less than a foot high with up to a dozen reddish-pink trumpet-like flowers, it's a real show stopper. Given an open location on well drained soil it only lasts for a couple of years, but price permits inexpensive replenishment. They can be ordered from Van Bourgondien, a good free catalog to have on hand.

The hardy Geraniums, *Geranium maculatum*, not to be confused with the commercial sun-loving plant, and

Virginia Blue Bells, *Mertensia virginica*, fall in the category of shade-loving plants, and, with a few others, provide May gardens with the same lush color produced in April.

This is also the month of Roses, especially the once-a-year blooming climbers and shrub trees. See the chapter on Roses for further description.

Among the climbers of vines we have *Clematis montana*, a native of China, introduced in 1900, and one of the best for this month. Quick growing and loaded with multitudes of truly breathtaking white to pink flowers, they preview others to come in June.

May Work Schedule

Brief mention was made in April of the importance of pruning shrubs and trees after they complete their blooming cycle, to keep them down to size. But pruning now is so important for all ornamentals that it bears repetition; it must be done before the end of spring, and in time for the plant to reconstruct its flower and/or fruiting buds for the following year. Later pruning of late winter and spring blooming shrubs and trees would affect their blooming and fruiting sequence.

Pruning during the three months of spring has many advantages. Not only can we gauge how much should be removed to keep the plant in scale, but normally during that period the insects are active, and as each portion comes under our scrutiny, we can analyze whether or not it needs spraying. Keeping plants open and aerated minimizes pest invasion as most insects seek dark corners in which to harbor and reproduce.

Another most important benefit,

seldom mentioned yet most realistic, is that in reducing its overall top surface, you are concentrating the plant's root strength, thus avoiding the need for excess amounts of fertilizer to keep it in balance. Before the popularity of fertilizers grew through advertising, old gardeners called this fertilizing through the pruning shears. And you know that makes sense.

In this day and age, when conservation of our natural resources is so critical, think of the surplus growth, if properly processed, as one of the best compost builders. To this end, few gardens can afford not to have a compost grinder, if only for economic reasons. It would be shameful for all of this debris not to find its way back into our own gardens, rather than on the garbage truck. In my own case, over the thirty years during which I have practiced this in my three acre garden, I have built up over a thousand square feet of rich land a foot deep in a low tidal portion of the area.

Perhaps most important, pruning teaches us the extensive potential of shaping plants into forms of our own fantasy, promoting an arching branch here and an opening there. Plan your dream garden with that in mind, and you will find that pruning becomes an adventure, not a drudgery. What better time to perform your art than after each plant in your landscape has climaxed its annual flowering performance.

May is a most important month in keeping unwanted weeds in check since normally the first crop is now going to seed. Don't rely too much on weed killers, even those which are supposedly selective, except, perhaps in regard to lawns.

We do know, however, that good lawns must be kept weed free and adequately fertilized. Fertilizing is complex as manufacturers constantly invent new formulas, and it is most important to choose a brand compatible to your soil and environment. Here, I would advise you to seek professional aid for the most current and appropriate product. Experimental stations or local golf courses are good sources for this information.

In most of Zone 8, this is the time of the year to raise your lawnmower's cutting height, normally from one inch to two inches, so that the individual grass plants will function better. I also recommend that to keep grass healthy and in good growth, it should have at least one half inch of water per week, whether in the form of natural rain or irrigation. This brings to mind two very important questions as far as all plants are concerned: how do we know when there has been adequate rainfall, and how can we compute our own watering schedules.

It may be said that because plant substances are ninety percent water, that the same percentage is required at all times for their well being. True enough. If the average rainfall in Zone 8 were equally divided and soaked into the ground, we would not need to supplement the plants' need for moisture. However, hard facts show that the weather does not always satisfy the demands of plants since much of the natural rainfall comes in the form of hard showers which are often wasted in run-offs. Also, rainfall often comes at times when plants cannot avail themselves of it.

Therefore, the real criteria in meeting plants' needs must be calculated on a week-to-week basis, in which temperatures and evaporation are tabulated. For instance in the British Isles, where temperatures are seldom as high as our own and where most of the precipitation comes in the form of drizzles, the same plant would need half as much water as it would here.

The only sure way of meeting a garden's need in so far as water is concerned, is to have it equipped with a rain gauge. This can be as simple as a straight-sided jar or glass placed in the garden where it will not be influenced by drips from trees or other baffle. It should be read at least once a week on the same day, considering one inch as the desired average. In other words, if it rains one inch a week that is sufficient even in the hot summertime. If not, the garden should be supplemented up to that amount. Note that I proposed only one-half inch for lawns.

It is also important to remember that if you have two inches in natural precipitation in one week, it does not follow that this is enough for two weeks. Plants do not operate this way as they do not have a camel's stomach. Because of ever-present plant transpiration, each day is different and conditions constantly vary, especially if plants are in the proximity of trees, which naturally rob lesser plants of surface moisture. Whichever way you figure it, moisture is one of the main requisites of a plant's normal growth.

There is still much to be learned about the role of moisture in gardening. My experiments in tidal gardening and mist irrigation are fascinating and involved enough to fill another book. My many years as a plain dirt gardener have convinced me that this phase of gardening has only reached its infancy, with most of the results being dis-

covered by you and me.

June

June is well suited to be the traditional month of brides, for as we will note, so many fine trees, shrubs, and perennials surface in their full glory. With this in mind, it might be well that all parents celebrate the birth of their first baby girl by planting a seedling, *Cornus kousa,* which is the Oriental counterpart to our native flowering Dogwood. It grows about the same size as ours and blooms approximately a month later with the same dramatic effect, except that its flower bracts are pointed instead of rounded and appear after the foliage is fully formed. Its slow growth will parallel a childhood, and within a score of years it will make a lovely overhead canopy for a wedding: another reminder that we should always plan for the future.

Also called Japanese Dogwood in the trade, *Cornus kousa* not only rivals our native species in looks, but, except for its rate of growth, is superior. It stays in bloom longer, at least five weeks, and as its fading flowers turn from pure white to a rusty pink, its

Oriental Dogwood, *Cornus kousa.* National Arboretum photo.

foliage gradually turns to autumn tints, earlier than our native tree. Both are compatible and make a wonderful combination. *Cornus kousa* was introduced in America around 1907 by the late E. H. Wilson, the great plant explorer who also brought us the famous Kurume Azaleas from Japan.

Oleander, *Nerium,* is one of the most popular plants of the deep south, originating from the Orient and Mediterranean region as well as certain tropical islands. It is grown in most of Zone 8 except its coolest limits, where it can do well if properly cultivated. I introduced it to the Norfolk parks around 1940, and plants of that vintage are now twenty feet tall, having withstood its coldest winters.

One method that may help in pushing it farther north into cooler regions is to set out new plants with a two or three year old root stock, as I have found that young plants will seldom survive the first winter. Certainly it is worthy of cultivation, and I feel sure that gardeners in Atlanta and other cities of the outer limits of Zone 8 can enjoy these beautiful plants.

As a matter of fact the same holds true for certain other subtropical plants such as the Eucalyptus, *Eucalyptus gunni,* and certain species of the hardy Palms, one of which, the Windmill Palm, *Trachycarpus chamaerops,* has withstood the Norfolk temperatures. The progeny of these when propagated from seeds are hardier than even the parent, according to Dr. Fletcher, former director of the Edinburgh Botanic Gardens in Scotland.

As we are ever seeking for new worlds to conquer in the realm of plants the three genera, Oleander, Eucalyptus, and Palms, offer an unusual challenge

to gardeners in Zone 8.

The main attributes of Oleanders are their long blooming season and ability to withstand drought conditions. Easily propagated, they can be rooted in water, placed in a four or five inch pot, and made to bloom as house plants, if they are afforded plenty of sun. Their color ranges from white to deep red. A few varieties are yellow and many of them are fragrant. Galveston, Texas, has adapted it as its city flower and emblem, and is the home of the National Oleander Society as well as perhaps one of the largest collections in America.

It is important to know that Oleanders are poisonous plants if eaten by humans or animals, although this is seldom noted by those who encourage it as an ornamental. In southern California, where it is much used, it has undergone research and many varieties have been developed. Nurseries often record them under variety names and sell a petite series of dwarf Oleanders in numerous colors, including salmon. Apparently their toxic foliage and other portions have not affected their popularity there.

The native Loblolly Bay, *Gordonia lasianthus,* not to be confused with *Gordonia alatamaha,* commonly called the Franklinia or Benjamin Franklin Tree, starts blooming about mid-May, and will continue to produce throughout the summer white fragrant blossoms which are not unlike our native Dogwood flower. There the resemblance stops since the Loblolly Bay is an evergreen which grows to fifty feet in its native habitat from southern Virginia to Florida and Mississippi. I believe that it is the finest small tree that grows, yet I know of no

Loblolly Bay, *Gordonia lasianthus.*

outlet for it commercially.

I have tried to popularize it by growing five hundred and distributing them through the Men's Garden Club of Tidewater, Virginia, and offering cuttings to local nurseries. Yet all who see it in bloom in my yard at this time of the year ask where to get it. I find it very easy to propagate, although it cannot be considered a fast grower, especially in its initial stages.

I first saw the Loblolly Bay in the higher portions of the Dismal Swamp in North Carolina growing, unhampered, by the acre. At the same time, it was being bulldozed down to make room for land development. It remains an enigma to me that such a valuable ornamental with its beautiful shiny foliage similar to the Bay Tree's has not captivated the interest of nurseries.

I do not know how much farther north than Norfolk, Virginia, it will

grow because I have failed to interest the trade. Therefore I hope that this mention of it will kindle interest, as the Loblolly Bay deserves to be better known and used. It flowers best exposed to the full sun, although the one in my yard is partially shaded.

Gordonia Franklinia is equally scarce, and the few nurseries who offer it get quite a price for it, often as much as twenty dollars for a three foot tree. It is presented as the lost tree from along the Alatamaha River in Georgia, discovered by John Bartram, the famous early plant collector, in 1770. He brought it to his garden in Philadelphia and named it in honor of his friend Benjamin Franklin. For some strange reason it was never found again in the wild, and all of its progeny have come to us from those originally collected by Bartram, either from seeds or cuttings.

Unlike *Gordonia lasianthus* it is deciduous, and its blooms are white with a yellow center three inches in diameter. Blooming in September and October, one of its main features is its autumn foliage color, which turns red and orange from a pale green. It too grows to twenty feet or more and makes a beautiful small pyramidal tree. The two are mentioned at this time as examples of some of our most beautiful flora which are not always well known. During the Bicentennial year a scramble for the Franklinia was made, with few plants available for distribution. Let us hope this will be remedied by the trade.

Another show stopper in June is the Goldenrain Tree, *Koelreuteria paniculata,* one of the best of the medium-sized flowering shade trees in existence. It is a native of China and grows to twenty-five feet in a globular

Goldenrain Tree, *Koelreuteria.*

form with bipinnated foliage. Its bright yellow flowers give it the name and appearance of golden rain. The flowers are soon followed by bladder-like pods, which are most attractive and furnish the seeds from which it is readily propagated. Another enigma of the plant kingdom is that it is not more widely available, although many nurseries do keep it in stock.

Just prior to the appearance of the Goldenrain Tree is the Goldenchain Tree, *Laburnum cytisus,* whose long golden clusters resemble the blooms of the Wisteria in form. A native of southern Europe and western Asia, this deciduous tree grows to twenty-five feet and prefers limestone soil. Only a few nurseries offer it in the trade, but it is worthwhile seeking as an unusual specimen.

The southeast prizes its Cape Jasmine, *Gardenia jasminoides,* which derived its common name from the misconception that it originated from the Cape of Good Hope in South Africa, whereas it is actually a native of China. Truly a magnificent evergreen, it grows to six feet with glossy foliage

and exotic scented white flowers. It blossoms best in full sunshine although it will stand some shade. In our cooler areas, where temperatures sometimes go to zero, it should be grown in a sheltered area. Perhaps most failures with this are due to the white fly, which lowers its resistance. As the Cape Jasmine is a host plant for this insect, consult your local authority for the proper spray program.

Some years ago a most successful grower of these evergreens gave me this recipe: spray with Volk oil early in the spring before the flies hatch and can be seen as white specks under the new foliage. Fertilize with half cottonseed meal and half bone meal about that time, using a cup of each to a four foot plant. Sprinkle the mixture around its base and water it in well. After it completes its blooming, prune to encourage new growth from the base.

The Sweetbay Magnolia, *Magnolia virginiana,* ranks high among our finest native small trees as its fragrance permeates the air in early summer. It is another valuable evergreen from our eastern seaboard which seems to be overlooked for the home landscape. It will grow to fifty or more feet high but is not overpowering, and will fit into most environments, taking most kindly to heavy pruning, if need be. Its small foliage is two-toned and nearly white underneath. Unlike *Magnolia grandiflora* it has small, white flowers, whose fruit pods are most effective in the fall.

I can think of no finer counterpart to the Sweetbay Magnolia among its deciduous native neighbors than the Sourwood, *Oxydendrum arboreum.* It too has been much neglected as it performs beautifully during the early summer from the time when it is forming its Lily-of-the-Valley-like white flowers to the fall when the seed capsules are nearly as attractive. By then its foliage begins to turn crimson, creating the first autumn effect in the landscape and tenaciously remaining until late fall. In Zone 8 where it abounds, Sourwood honey is sold as a delicacy, and the natives place their beehives in proximity to the trees while they are in bloom. Truly a beautiful and most useful tree, it grows to fifty feet but can be held confined and grown in planters as a feature on terraces, as I saw it featured at the National Arboretum in Washington, D. C.

Sourwood Tree, *Oxydendrum arboreum*. National Arboretum photo.

It is unfortunate that the Mimosa, *Albizzia julibrissin,* so prevalent within our zone and beyond, is subject to the Mimosa wilt, for which there is no known remedy. Even the so-called wilt-resisting strains such as Tryoon seem to succumb to it. There is no small shade tree that can ever take its place as a flowering ornamental with its powder-puff-like pink blossoms. But I feel confident that some immune strain will soon be found.

The Chinese Chestnut, *Castanea mollissima,* is slowly replacing our American Chestnut, *C. dentata,* which was the finest tree on the North American continent until it fell prey to the Chestnut blight over fifty years ago. The Chinese Chestnut is highly recommended not only for its edible nuts but as a wonderful flowering shade tree growing in a globular form of fifty or more feet. It blooms at this time of the year and is now available in many nurseries.

If I were limited to one flowering evergreen shrub, without a qualm I would choose *Abelia*. The reasons are obvious; it will tolerate shade and sun, no known insects or disease will attack it, and it is available in several species. Like many of our other better shrubs and trees, it originates from China and Japan. The one most often grown is *Abelia grandiflora,* which in our zone will grow ten or more feet, with thousands of small pink flowers in clusters produced consistently throughout the summer, then replaced with seed capsules which are equally attractive. By then its evergreen foliage turns to autumn tints, making it attractive at all seasons.

There are smaller species of this genus, notably *A. edward goucher,* which grows only to five feet or so and has lavender-purple flowers, and *A. schumanni,* which has lavender-pink flowers. All of these make up into beautiful hedges and are recommended as such.

Another shrub notable for its resistance to disease and insects is Nandina, *Nandina domestica,* often referred to as the Chinese Sacred Bamboo. The flowers are in large, white clusters, followed by berries which hang in Grape-like fashion and turn to deep crimson from Thanksgiving throughout the winter.

Nandinas are evergreen with foliage made up of leaflets, which likewise turn crimson during winter, making this season the climax of its beauty. The plant itself will grow to eight to ten feet unless pruned annually to allow its young Bamboo-like shoots to replace the old. This should be done on or before April to keep it down to half its matured size. There are yellow berried clones of Nandina, but they have not proven as popular.

Nandinas prefer being grown in the full open sun although they will tolerate half shade, as well as very dry locations, as found in dry sandy areas. I know such locations are hard to cope with, so let me now mention a good companion plant, the Santolinas, *Santolina chamaecyparissus,* commonly called Lavender Cotton. They are actually herbs which produce button-like yellow blossoms that contrast most attractively against its grey or green foliage, as it is available in both shades.

Santolina is an excellent ground cover or border plant, growing to only twelve to eighteen inches high with a spread of the same dimensions. Its main requisite is well-drained soil, and once it is established will not require any watering. At this time of the year after flowering, it is best to shear it back to maintain its compactness, otherwise it sprawls and loses its usefulness to supress weeds.

While searching for plants that will stand drought and hard to fill places, we automatically think of Yucca, *Yucca filamentosa,* also known under the common name of Adam's Needle or Spanish Bayonet. This most useful evergreen is available in many species with the smaller one, *Y. filamentosa,* native to our southern states. The Spanish Dagger or Gloriosa grows to eight or ten feet high and often repeats its flowering habit. There are also new hybrids available with variegated foliage. Whatever type you prefer, they stand out in the landscape with their single stemmed trunk and spiked fronds suggesting a desert scene, although they will grow almost anywhere, even where it is wet, provided they are afforded lots of sunlight.

In that same category are the Prickly Pears, *Opuntia,* which you will never forget if you ever encounter them growing wild along the seashore. There are many species and most of them are thorny, with beautiful flowers which develop into edible fruits, well known to the Indians. Considerable interest has been shown in growing them as cattle food in arid countries. This all points to one fact; nature provides plants for all contingencies and if you are interested in seashore or Cactus gardens, *Opuntias* should be included in your research.

June brings out great varieties and species of Hydrangeas. Native from Georgia to Florida and Mississippi, the

Oakleaf Hydrangea, *Hydrangea quercifolia*, grows to eight feet, and produces panicles of white flowers, which, along with its foliage, turn lovely autumn shades in the fall.

However, we are more familiar with *H. macrophylla hortensis*, known in the trade as the French or Florist Hydrangea, and a native of Japan. We see it around Easter as a potted plant with pink blossoms which turn blue when planted in our average garden soil. It changes color when the pH factor varies from neutral to acid. If we wish to keep it pink, we add lime and bonemeal to the soil, but to intensify the blue we can use acidifiers.

Hydrangeas require adequate moisture to keep them in a good state of growth. As there are many species, careful study is needed to find the shrubs best suited to fill our landscape theme.

Other Hydrangeas worthy of note for this season are the *H. arborescens* variety, Anabella, which remains white irrespective of soil, and the *H. acuminata* variety, Pink Beauty, which is most attractive and long blooming. Also of merit are the Lace-Cap Hydrangeas, which are somewhat flatheaded with an outer rim of open flowers varying from pink to blues. All of these will average four feet in height

My wife, Florrie, admires the *Hydrangea quercifolia.*

unless otherwise controlled through pruning.

Relatively unknown to many gardeners are the Hypericums, sometimes sold under the name of St. Johnswort or Aaron's Beard, which bloom throughout June and often repeat later. Several types and species are available. The better known is *H. calycinum*, a wonderful ground cover growing less than a foot. It is evergreen and produces a multitude of bright yellow flowers three inches in diameter. The foliage turns golden in the fall. A shrubby variety, *Hidcote*, grows to three feet and was developed in England as a small evergreen shrub or low hedge.

The name Hibiscus applies to a large genus of plants of which the species are often confused, such as *H. syriacus*, which is sold in the trade as an Althaea. The true Althaeas include the perennial Hollyhock and Marsh Mallow. Even as amateurs, we should keep the true names in perspective.

H. syriacus or Shrubby Althaea is a native of China and India, and since its introduction in 1790 has been hybridized and crossed to bring out many fine varieties, most growing to over ten feet. The Blue Bird is a fine example of the beauty of this genus and a most recent one, Diane, brought out by the National Arboretum, is a pure white interspecific hybrid well worth searching for.

The main characteristic of the Hibiscus is its long flowering quality, blooming consistently for several months during our hot summers. This deciduous shrub should be pruned annually between the new year and April to keep it furnished with new stems on which flowers are formed.

Many fine and worthy perennials

Althaea Diane, *Hibiscus syriacus.*

can grace our gardens at this time, such as the Japanese Iris which was noted last month. Another, the common Shasta Daisy, has come a long way from the wild species in the field to the striking cut flowers of today. The *Chrysanthemum maximum* variety, Alaska, is one of the best, with thirty to thirty-six inch long stiff stems. It is a glistening white with prominent yellow stamens and it blooms all of June into July.

A wild plant that grows in southern Europe, whose foliage was the model for the ornamentation atop Corinthian columns, is the classical Acanthus. This perennial has glossy foliage growing to two feet and white, overlaid with pink, flower spikes in

June reaching over three feet. It can be raised from the *Acanthus mollis* seed. Needing to be sheltered from the western sun, it remains evergreen under normal winters in our zone. I consider it one of my better plants, aside from its classical connection, but do not like its common name, Bear's Breech.

Yarrow, *Achillea,* a wild flower from southern Europe, deserves a prominent place in the early summer border, especially if you select the variety Coronation Gold. It produces large umbels on two-foot stems that can be cut and kept for dried arrangements, lasting for the entire year. It prefers a sunny location to intensify its striking color.

June is the month when climbing vines can be exhibited, but none will outdo Clematis, of which there are over fifty species in cultivation with many varieties. For a selection you must really resort to those firms who specialize in their production as most of them are grafted plants. *C. lanuginosa can-*

White Clematis climbing along my garden fence.

dida, for instance, is a white variety with six to eight inch flowers which bloom consistently the entire summer. Each blossom is a showpiece all of its own when allowed to climb up a six to eight foot trellis. Others with exquisite coloring hard to describe deserve your consideration.

Through judicious selection, Lilies can dominate the open perennial border. Because they are a sophisticated genus, reaching us from all over the world and from many climates, we must select them through the guidance of those who have had experience with their local response. In most of our zone the Easter Lily offered by the florist can be planted out in the garden and will repeat year after year around June. One of the most persistent Lilies for the garden is the Regale strain, introduced from China around 1910. This marvelous white Lily has since been crossed with others and seems to resist many of the diseases which attack Lily bulbs. Since good bulbs are expensive, my recommendation is that you thoroughly explore their potential in your immediate area.

After over twenty years of experience in my own garden, under the best circumstances, I have only a few strains that have survived the vicissitudes of soil and climatic conditions, to which they are most sensitive. While Daylilies cannot replace the Regale Lily in the sophisticated world of plants; they can, however, best serve the average gardener's budget and effort.

In our portion of the growing world, anticipating the torrid days of July and August, we must recognize that since few plants are capable of standing the long and high average

Lilies.
National Arboretum photo.

temperatures, those few that can should be carefully analyzed to complete our color schemes. Fortunately many of the June performers repeat in later months, and if special care is necessary, will be discussed in the appropriate month.

June Work Schedule

Perhaps the most demanding plants in our gardens are the Hybrid Tea Roses and their relatives, especially because of the inroad of black-spot and other pests at a time when they are growing best and normally producing the most. We refer you to the chapter on Roses as a timely reminder.

Another reminder is to keep sowing vegetable seeds, as those sown in early spring are now being harvested. Again, I refer you to our vegetable section, particularly the sowing chart. One of the least observed rules in getting the most out of a given piece of ground is to sow only what we can harvest. Over-planting results not only in waste of seed, but energy and quality as well. Most vegetables soon lose their flavor and vitamins after reaching their peak.

Mid-year is the time to plant for our summer gardens. Most spring participants have completed their role and the early spring bulbs are in the process of building their corms below. I often wonder how Daffodils fare when meticulous gardeners braid their withered tops for a neater garden. At least it shows affection.

Personally, I would rather carefully plant a few seeds or small seedlings of a quickly maturing annual to hide the bulb's fading foliage. Have you ever thought about that? Sanvitalia, the persistent creeping Zinnia, will bloom for the rest of the summer and fall, and its tiny golden blossoms will be an excellent cover. Dozens of other annuals will do a similar job without interfering with the bulb's development.

June is a good time to sow most annuals, especially those with large seeds such as Marigolds—and what a flower that one is. Its many varieties offer a wide spectrum of color, from the most dwarf to the three foot giants.

Consider also the many summer bulbs that can be purchased at this time. All you need is a trip to your favorite garden shop—or let your fingers walk through some of the colorful catalogs.

July

The hot sultry days of July turn Zone 8 into a veritable Tropics, sending most gardeners to seek relief under the spreading limbs of shade trees. This tropical atmosphere should serve to remind us that many of the lush flora of more southern regions will flourish in our heat.

And in seeking trees for our summer shade, every gardener in Zone 8 should consider the Crapemyrtle, *Lagerstoemia indica.* It not only grows into a delicate tree for the small garden, but can be pruned as a shrub; both will provide you with a profusion of flowers during our area's hottest months.

The Crapemyrtle was introduced around 1747, via western Europe from China, and of course needs no introduction to most of us. In certain areas it has escaped cultivation even to the extent of reseeding itself. Recently the Japanese seed trade released a dwarf clone of mixed colors, which they call an annual variety. It actually behaves more like a perennial and will be worth watching as a new addition to this fine shrub.

It is said that Crapemyrtles bloom for over a hundred days, and this is true when viewed collectively. Individually, however, much depends on how they are pruned and cared for. In Tidewater, Virginia, we have featured them as street plantings, with one street over a mile long having over a thousand trees fifteen to twenty feet tall and touching one another although

Crapemyrtle.

planted fifteen feet apart more than thirty years ago. They present color from July Fourth to Labor Day.

Crapemyrtles are best grown when allowed to develop naturally into a small multistemmed tree. You will get better quality flowers if they are annually pruned by thinning the inner growth out, permitting the sunlight to penetrate their superstructure. Longer flowering periods will result from cutting back their flower heads after they have completed their first flush of blooms, as they will immediately produce another crop. This technique is time consuming, but rewarding if followed.

While Crapemyrtles will grow in most any type of soil, they will do better if the soil is of average fertility, and will respond to an annual application of 5-10-5 fertilizer at the rate of one cup per foot of height, applied in mid-April to stimulate their new growth. Twenty years after planting, some trees may need more intensive feeding as evidenced by a crop of flowers diminishing in size and amount. When this happens, the trees should be fertilized by starting three feet from the trunk and drilling twelve to eighteen inch deep holes two feet apart in a circular pattern, terminating a foot beyond the diameter of the top spread.

The fertilizer should be a mixture of three cupsful of 5-10-5 fertilizer in a twelve quart bucket of topsoil, which is used to refill the holes. There are also mechanical ways of placing plant food in the soil through water pressure which are especially effective since all types of feeding should be followed by adequate watering.

It is doubtful, however, that those originally planted at Middleton Garden in South Carolina over two hundred years ago and still thriving were ever afforded this luxury. This emphasizes their tenacity, which makes them undoubtedly the finest flowering ornamental coming to us from the Orient.

I hope that this reminder of the Crapemyrtle will help keep us from taking them too much for granted in an area that grows them so well, and I encourage all Zone 8 gardeners to feature them collectively wherever possible so that areas that are not fortunate enough to grow them will know that we care a great deal for the heritage of this species. The National Arboretum in Washington, D.C., has done considerable research in improving varieties and colors, and would welcome your inquiries.

Yes, July is the time to consider shade trees for fall planting. Every time I travel through what is left of rural Tidewater, I marvel at the foresight of the early settlers who carefully selected and transplanted Willow Oaks, *Quercus phellos*, from our forests to act as shade and accent trees to their dwellings. Many have survived more than two centuries of hurricanes and severe weather conditions to grace the lawns of more modern homes. Conversely, poorly selected trees are not only a nuisance, but a very expensive one at that. As an old forester, I estimate that tree removal costs as much as two to three dollars per year of the tree's existence.

There is no reason to let a tree become a liability, because much research has produced varieties of each genus to satisfy any need. However, it is no longer practical to order or purchase a tree by its family name, because there are so many different types and forms available.

Let us take the Maple, *Acer,* family for instance. From the Norway species, *Acer platanoides,* a tree named Summershade has been developed which is heat resistant and would be ideal for Zone 8. There is also one called *Acer ginnala* which has a dense compact growth habit to fit in close quarters of twenty feet or more. If you want a rare and interesting small tree, *Acer griseum* has bark which resembles River Birch, giving it the name Paperbark Maple.

The Locust, *Robinia,* whose wood is synonymous with durability, has also evolved to new forms and textures in the species *Gleditsia.* The offspring of this species are so sophisticated that many have been given patents, for example the thornless Shademaster. Among its many qualifications the Shademaster resists droughts and is free from disease. It readily transplants, and is quick to grow into a straight trunk with ascending branches. Unlike its ancestors, it holds its foliage until late fall, and is deep-rooted enough to allow grass to grow at its base. Perhaps its most favorable feature is its lacy foliage through which filtered sunlight easily penetrates.

Another clone of *Gleditsia* is Sunburst; in the fall it bears golden bronze foliage up to the last eight or ten inches of the leaf tip which turns a brilliant yellow. Another is Rubylace, whose spring foliage color resembles the purple tones of some of the Japanese Cut-Leaf Maples, but then turns to a glossy green as the leaves mature. The Locusts certainly deserve your scrutiny.

Ginkgo biloba, occassionally described as the Maidenhair Tree, and one of the few surviving the glacial period, is perhaps the most immune to insects and diseases. It is now available as a grafted male, which bears no fruit and thus eliminates the unpleasant odor. The beautiful fall coloring of the Ginkgo makes it one of the most valuable shade trees for our zone.

Lindens, *Tilia,* have long been grown in this country and in old New York were called Lime Trees by the Dutch settlers. The native species, *Tilia americana,* is found throughout our northern hemisphere but is not as desirable as the small leaf Linden, *Tilia cordata,* from Europe. Greenspire is one of the best of these, and although patented and therefore more expensive, a long term investment of great value. It has inherited the spicy fragrance of its ancestors, which may be the origin of its old nickname, the Lime Tree. This fragrance during its flowering period draws honey bees which have made the tree famous for Linden honey. From my boyhood I well remember the tea made from the leaves of Lindens, grown and processed in Germany.

A list of summer shade trees could not be complete without mention of at least one member of the graceful Willow family. I have chosen to recommend the Corkscrew Willow, *Salix matsudana tortuosa,* because of its unusual twisted spiraling branches which look as if they have received a permanent wave.

Blooming with the first heat of summer is the Chaste Tree, *Vitex,* whose two main species are *Agnuscastus,* from southern Europe and western Asia, and *Negundo* from Northern China and Korea. Both are deciduous, grow to fifteen feet, and produce spikes of pale violet, a ro-

The flowers of the Chaste Tree, *Vitex agnuscastus*. National Arboretum photo.

mantic flower along grey foliage. They were introduced here in the mid-1700s, yet are not as popular as they deserve to be. There is a pink and white variety of *Vitex agnuscastus* which is most desirable. All of them give a tropical appearance in the garden landscape at a time of the year when flowering shrubs are at a premium. They should be severely pruned each spring to produce better flowering spikes.

Another good plant to incorporate in this setting is the Butterfly Bush, *Buddleia davidi,* also called Summer Lilac and aptly so because of its fragrance. These are available in named varieties which more or less describe their color such as Black Knight, Empire Blue, Purple Prince, and White Profusion. They come to us from the Himalayas, and were developed in England where the summers are cooler, and therefore they enjoy a well-aerated place in the landscape, preferably shaded from the hot afternoon sun. They prefer the cooler days and nights of autumn and will bloom until frost if you keep the spent flower

heads cut off. The long spiked flowers attract butterflies and this combination lends animation to the setting. They are best cut back to within a foot of the ground after completing their blooming sequence in late fall, and will provide four months of enjoyment a year. In other words, I have found them best handled as a shrubby perennial, although they will grow to over six feet in one season.

Growing along damp areas, a small shrub aptly called Summersweet, *Clethra alnifolia*, may attract you by its fragrance. Native of our eastern seaboard, it produces pink flower spikes which vary to pure white when growing in the wild. These flower spikes fade out to small seed pods, which explains why it is known to the natives in some parts of the south as a Sweet-pepper Bush. A most delightful deciduous plant with attractive foliage, it will tolerate half shade and grow to around four feet.

Many perennials can be counted on to perform during July such as the stately Marsh Mallow, also known as the Rose Mallow, *Hibiscus moscheutos*. There is a native species that grows

Butterfly Bush's spikey blossom, *Buddleia davidi*. National Arboretum photo.

along our brackish marshes, but will grow just as well on high land if kept adequately moist. They produce flowers to ten inches in diameter, of white to light pink. From these hybrids two good selections are Clown and Southern Belle, which is a blush pink with a red eye. They should not be confused with the Rose of Sharon mentioned last month, nor the tropical *H. rosa sinensis*, which grows prolifically in Florida and can be grown here as tubed specimens and wintered indoors. This entire family is most spectacular for the summer garden.

I refer from time to time to certain plants which by nature are nomadic because their natural method of spreading is through their seeds. One of these is the Harlekin Glory-Bower, *Clerodendron trichotomum*, originally from eastern China; it migrated here around 1880, and apparently never has stopped looking for a new home. It grows to be a small tree of twenty-five feet and during July produces clusters of fragrant white blossoms which permeate the area, followed by turquoise blue berries with a red calix. These berry clusters, which perhaps gave it its nickname of Harlekin, soon attract birds which distribute them around for a surprise crop the following spring. While it may be classified as a weedy tree, Harlekin is a most delightful one and if you do not have it, is worth introducing to your area. The seedlings will normally bloom the third year, at which time it should be about six feet high. Although it has a rather short life span of twelve to fifteen years, its many progeny continue blooming.

Another member of that genus is *Clerodendron bungei*, which is best treated as a perennial. It too spreads freely through underground runners, producing rosy-purple clusters of blossoms which are not fragrant. I must warn you that they will take over unless restricted. But where space is not at a premium, they are welcome nomads.

When the first settlers came to the North American continent they found many species of what we call Black-Eyed-Susans, *Rudbeckia hirta*, blooming at this time of the year. The European gardeners prized this flower and about twenty-five years ago introduced a cultivated clone listed as Rudbeckia variety Goldstrum. This one takes the spotlight in my yard and will do so even as it has shed its last petal in October, exhibiting only its jet-black cone.

The parent plant will withstand severe droughts and even impoverished soil, and still grow to thirty inches, consistently throwing up new wiry stems which hold those golden blossoms with black centers. A standout in the summer landscape, it is without doubt one of our best carefree perennials. From this clan, American hybridizers have also produced the Gloriosa Daisy, which should also be included in our summer display.

Clerodendron bungei.

A sure way to attract attention in your garden is to plant the California Poinciana, *Poinciana gilliesi*, and surprise your visitors with its tropical appearance. Hardier than its Florida counterpart, the Bird of Paradise as it is commonly called, it is a native of India, will grow to about ten to twelve feet, and produce bright yellow flowers. It is not common in cultivation but is offered in west coast garden centers and nurseries. It can be grown from seed and because it requires some protection in our climate, prefers full sun on the south side of a building.

An evergreen shrub which should be better recognized is *Eurya japonica*, sometimes sold as *Cleyera japonica*, and a native of eastern Asia. At this time of the year it produces white blossoms, which are followed by small black fruit. Its main attraction as a shrub is its glossy foliage, which looks as if each of its three to four inch leaves has been varnished; some will turn deep bronze in the fall. Although rather slow of growth, it eventually reaches five to six feet and makes a beautiful hedge. It is well worth searching for.

In mid-July the Japanese Pagoda

Poinciana gilliesi peeps over a rustic fence in Richmond, Virginia. National Arboretum photo.

Tree, *Sophora japonica*, also referred to as the Chinese Scholar Tree, comes into bloom. This deciduous tree grows to over fifty feet and has green pinnate leaves, averaging nine inches in length and composed of about twelve elliptic leaflets. It normally does not bloom until it attains thirty years of age and then bears panicles of creamy white, Pea-shaped flowers. There are other species, but this one is the most beautiful and perhaps the rarest, as it is seldom sold in commerce.

July Work Schedule

We have reached the peak of our daylight spans, and believe it or not, plants react to the change from maximum photosynthesis to increasing shadows. Devotees of Chrysanthemums know that within this month the last pinching is required to develop a nice branching plant and that those intended as single stem specimens will need staking and careful disbudding to produce those large heads. Besides that, as soon as the flower buds begin to form, feeding with a special Mum formula is in order.

Be sure to raise the cutting height on your mower if you aspire to a Blue Grass or Fescue lawn. This will not be necessary if you are dealing with Bermuda. In fact we are entering Bermuda weather, and it is time to sow the seed or sprig it as the case may be. Be sure to consult a local authority if you are trying to rebuild an old turf or start a new one.

I need not remind you that while July normally enjoys the highest rainfall in the calendar, it is the time when plants require it most. All of them, including the lawn, must have at least an inch a week, and gardeners must

Pinching at this stage will anticipate and prevent later pruning.

August

Were it not for the many in our floral kingdom, August a drab color month. Some of th the Crapemyrtle, Oleanders, Hib Abelias, and others previously n tioned. And although not a true repeater, *Hydrangea tardiva,* a member of the June-blooming species, is kind enough to wait until the hot days of August to open its cool blue flowers.

However, nature was not entirely thoughtless and provided us with the Sedums, a large family of succulents that are generally overlooked by the home gardener for places other than the rock garden.

Withstanding most any growing condition, including poor and arid soil, the Sedums, commonly called Stone-

make up the deficiency if the rain gauge shows there is one. It's all very simple, but of course can be expensive when your water bill comes around.

Here are some figures which will exemplify this. It takes 27,143 gallons of water to deposit the equivalent of one inch of rain. The average cost from municipal sources is one dollar per thousand gallons. It can also be computed that half of the water required to sustain plants can be saved if the ground surface is adequately mulched to retard evaporation. Therefore, especially at this time of the year, it would pay to check how much insulation your garden surface has, for good mulch not only holds back ground water, but a half-inch to an inch of mulch will keep the ground surface cooler by at least five degrees. All of these factors are conducive to better growing conditions.

Mulching materials vary a great deal and should be gauged through their economic availability in your particular area. Pine needles, ground bark, peanut hulls, or any loose material will act as an insulator for the soil.

Dr. Charles Elstrodt and I examine *Hydrangea tardiva.*

71

Sedum decorates my driveway.

crops, actually seem to enjoy the hot days of August. Although some Sedums are annuals, the most spectacular is the perennial Japanese Stonecrop, *Sedum spectabile*. These come in many named varieties with Indian Chief, which grows to three feet and changes hues to bronze as it ages, serving as the best example of the versatility of the species. Others, such as the creeper Spurium Dragon's Blood, are also blooming at this time of the year.

On the opposite side of the growing scale is the Cardinal Flower, *Lobelia cardinalis*, found blooming in the shadows of rich woodland. A most stately, vivid red perennial, it grows to four feet on straight sturdy stems and requires a humid and consistently damp location. I first saw it in the mountains along the edge of a waterfall, carpeted with Maidenhair Fern, *Adiantum pedatum*. It left such an impression on me that I never stopped trying to establish it when I acquired a permanent home along the coast. I

finally did, and at this time of the year the Cardinal Flower is a beacon of color, and some place in your garden should be found for it.

Liriope or Lilyturf, *Liriope muscari*, is one of the most useful evergreen ground covers or border plants for southern gardens, and has also proven hardy to Long Island, New York. It blooms at this time of the year, producing short spikes of flowers, from the deep lavender of the Majestic variety to the pure white of the Monroe. It multiplies from underground rhizomes as well as seed and is most prolific, thriving under most garden situations including sun or shade, although it will grow and color better in the shade.

As a ground cover it grows to one foot and will overpower most weeds, including Nut-Grass, yet will allow interplanted bulbs such as Daffodils to penetrate.

Cotoneasters have acquired a bad reputation in southern gardens because of their susceptibility to fire blight, a devastating disease that attacks both Cotoneasters and Hawthorns in our humid south. However, the deciduous species of Cotoneasters such as *Cotoneaster divaricata*, which grows to six feet, and *D. apiculata*, a dwarf type to less than three feet, have survived in my garden for over twenty years. Their main contribution is the early coloring of their berries, which appear ahead of most other berried shrubs including the earliest Pyracanthas.

Another early berry bearer is the Bush Honeysuckle or Tartarian Honeysuckle, *Lonicera tatarica*, of which there are many varieties. Most of them originated at the Arnold Arboretum in Boston, which is a good indication of their hardiness. They are all deciduous and a great attraction in early spring while in flower; most are delightfully fragrant and a great attraction to birds. My philosophy has always been that if you want our feathered friends to help you keep down the insect population, you should provide them with an occasional dessert.

Another favorite of the bird kingdom which bears fruit this month is the Papaw Tree, *Asimina triloba*. For some reason it is seldom encountered in commerce or grown as an ornamental tree, and yet its fruit was a great delicacy to the Indians and it is hardy throughout our zone and north to Canada. It grows to about twenty feet with flowers of little significance, but its fruit, aromatic with a distinctive taste, attains the size and shape of small bananas. I have seen them growing in the North Carolina-Virginia area and cannot understand their scarcity unless it is due to difficulty in transplanting them. However, they can be readily raised from seed and will be fruit-producing trees within four years.

August Work Schedule

While most plants resent being disturbed at this time of the year, the Bearded or German Iris are an exception. Because of the nature of their growth habit from July to September this is the best time to work around them and reset them if necessary. This includes all Irises that have surface rhizomes.

The rhizomes are planted flat pointing downward and half covered with soil. They must not be buried as it is necessary for them to be sun-baked to produce the maximum number of flowers. This is one of the few plants that should not be mulched. However, it is a fallacy that Irises require poor soil; they will produce better flowers if the ground is adequately prepared.

The soil should be dug deeply and a little well-decayed manure worked into the subsoil. A quart of ground limestone and bonemeal should be incorporated into each square yard of topsoil. These slow-acting organic fertilizers will activate the new roots as they are being set and again in early spring as the new growth forms the flower stems. A cup of 5-10-5 fertilizer will complete the care cycle. If the rhizomes are set about a foot apart, these conditions should last them for three years before they require re-setting.

Bearded Iris will produce best in full sun in well-drained land, although I have seem them prosper at the edge of tidal lands, where they are occasionally flooded. Having had some experience in dealing with tidal waters, I wish to make this observation, which I can only rationalize through some sort of a sixth sense that gardeners acquire. The tides rise and fall twice a day and

Iris bulb—set at ground level. Barely cover rhizome and cut foliage to 6" fan.

when falling create a vacuum action, thereby forcing certain elements into the soggy soil, possibly an abundance of oxygen. Therefore plants like Iris, which normally only tolerate well-drained soil on high lands and would rot if that land was soggy, are conundrums in this case. I use the term soggy because tidal lands are normally in that condition when the elevation above high water is a foot or less. I have grown many plants in topsoil one foot above high water.

Flowering Senna, *Cassia corymbosa.*

September

You hardly expect shrubs to burst into bloom as we approach autumn, especially those with spectacular blossoms approaching that of the Forsythia in color and form, yet the Flowering Senna, *Cassia corymbosa,* a gift from the Argentine flora, does just that. I do not understand why it has not been better popularized because once established in the garden it will readily spread by seed, which it produces prolifically. Once in a while it will freeze back when temperatures go down below the teens, but will readily sprout back. I have distributed it through my community and it has made me many new friends.

It will grow to ten or twelve feet or can be kept to half that height by annual pruning as it blooms on the new wood. Flowering prolifically through September into October, its golden Pea-like blossoms look lovely over a ground cover of lavender Colchicums, which will bloom about the same period. You will enjoy anticipating this combination each year at this time. Of course, you can always use contrasting Mums,

the star performers at this time of the year.

When we mention Chrysanthemums, we start an entirely new subject on which volumes have been written. Only through careful study can we take advantage of their potential value and adapt them to our garden scheme. We can have them in bloom from late August to Thanksgiving and later in our zone, where we can grow anything from the exotic Spiders to that giant of flowers, the so-called Football Mum. I recommend writing to specialists in the Chrysanthemum business as many offer free catalogs, well illustrated in color with recommendations in their growing and time blooming sequence. This genus is perhaps the greatest investment you can make in the promotion of a fall garden.

One of the great mysteries of plant behavior is why the Ginger Lily, *Hedychium,* the garland flower of Hawaii, and a native of tropical India and China, has chosen to grow, thrive, and flower in the warmer sections of Zone 8, where the thermometer has tumbled to

Chrysanthemums brighten my front garden.

twelve degrees. It was introduced in southeast Virginia twenty years ago when I planted it out of doors purely by accident. And yet, on a recent trip to Hawaii where Ginger Lilies were growing in profusion, they were not any more prolific than those in my garden.

It is truly a grand gesture on the part of nature to let us share this magnificent perennial, which grows to four feet and produces a six to eight inch raceme of white, delightfully fragrant flowers at this time of the year, persisting in bloom into October. So do not be misguided by literature that says they only thrive in Florida and tropical America. They will die down in the winter but reproduce through fleshy rhizomes that grow as Iris do. I keep mine mulched with Pine straw not to push my luck. They like damp ground and revel at the edge of our tidal water.

Crinum Lilies are September bloomers which belie their semi-tropical origin, of which the best is the species *Powelli. Crinum longifolium,* with leaves a couple of feet long and tremendous bulbs reaching eight to ten inches in diameter, is the most common. Both are worthwhile growing for fall effect, although not normally offered for sale. They flower about the time *Montbretias* come into bloom with their miniature Gladiola-like spikes. Together with Lycoris, often sold as Hardy Amaryllis, *Lycoris squamigera,* this group of plants will all thrive and are worth seeking to impart a bit of the exotic to the fall landscape.

I became acquainted with *Serissa foetida,* for which I cannot find any listed common name, in a Chattanooga, Tennessee nursery. It was grown out of doors in a protected area, which surprised me as I have for many years considered it a conservatory plant. While it is not spectacular, with its tiny white flowers strung along its evergreen foliage and graceful willowy stems, I realized that it would make a most useful base planting shrub since it is dwarf and grows to only three feet. Nurseries are losing a good opportunity in not producing this plant for use as small hedges. This particular nursery in Chattanooga did not retail it for some reason or other. It is a native of Southeast Asia and listed as a tender plant for use in frost-free countries. It overwinters readily in Norfolk as an evergreen. Perhaps other cities in our zone will have equal luck in growing this plant.

September Work Schedule

With the return of cooler temperatures average garden work picks up momentum, and for those of us who like to propagate our own plants from cuttings, this is an ideal time. Home propagation can be as simple or as sophisticated as we wish. It is simple to take the tip growth from a hybrid

Tea Rose, after snipping off the faded flower, and make a cut below a leaf bud at least ten inches long. Strip off the foliage six inches above the cut, dip the stem in a root growing compound, and insert it in a four to six inch pot full of a prepared commercial sterilized potting and rooting compound.

The important part of this operation is to have the rooting medium adequately moist and well firmed around the stem of the cutting once inserted, then watered again to exclude all air-pockets that may have been left. The potted cutting is then placed in the shade, such as the north side of a dwelling, and covered by an inverted quart mason jar, which will act as a miniature greenhouse when it has been sealed by working the jar into the soil surface. Under those conditions, it normally will not require additional moisture until rooted, which takes place in a month to six weeks.

This same procedure can be used for other hardwood cuttings such as Azaleas, Camellias, Pyracanthas, Hollies, and others. Hollies, however, might require several months, and should be rooted in a self-contained

pot so that when you are ready to set them out you will not disturb the root system. Such plants are best left in the pot over the winter, but will need protection to prevent the frost from penetrating the pots. The procedure is simply to place Pine needles or other loose mulch over and around them.

This process can of course be augmented by using a cold frame as a miniature greenhouse for many pots. This is an old and foolproof method in which the rooting medium, the main agent, is kept in a state of animation until the cuttings are rooted.

The faster and newer method for rooting plants is the full sun exposure process, under mist, which requires sophisticated equipment such as time clock controls or what is called "Mistmatic," an aluminum leaf-like apparatus electronically controlled by prevailing moisture. This, however, costs hundreds of dollars for the original installation, a sum which will buy you a lot of young plants.

September and October are the best times of the year to renovate lawns, especially those using Fescues, Blue grass, and other cool weather

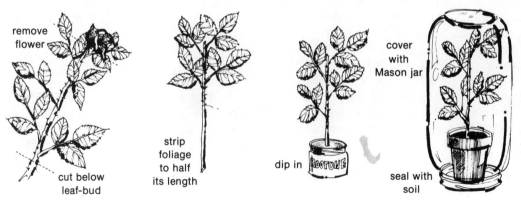

remove flower

cut below leaf-bud

strip foliage to half its length

dip in ROOTONE

cover with Mason jar

seal with soil

Propagating Roses.

grasses, discussed in detail under the chapter on lawns.

Another reminder, found under Camellia culture, is that this is the time for gibbing blooms to hasten the blooming period by several months.

Those of us who cannot develop Delphiniums because of our early summer high temperatures, should sow its near relative, the Larkspurs. By next May, they will produce beautiful spikes in colors according to your choice. They resent transplanting, so try to sow them directly where they are to bloom. If the spring space is unavailable at this time, sow them in pots. Wallflowers, another biennial, can be handled the same.

Cleaning up the perennial and other flower borders is urgent as we prepare to plant bulbs at this time. They are now generally available at the various garden centers and it is best to make your list and acquire them before they are picked over. Most of the spring bulbs have a protective skin and the main criterion in selecting a good viable bulb is to have that skin intact, especially on Tulip bulbs. Bulbs can be held over in a cool place and planted later, up to November, which is the preferred time for our zone.

Many of the so-called annuals and perennials to be used in dried arrangements should be picked while they are in their prime. I am thinking primarily of the lovely Sedum, Indian Chief, which is one to include in your shopping list if it is not already a garden occupant.

October

An inventory of October florescence reveals that most subjects are holdovers, or late flowering clones of those previously mentioned, showing that nature is cautious of approaching frosty nights. Some of the repeaters are the ever-blooming Roses, and if we have carefully catered to their well-being, they will amply reward us at fall Rose shows. However, the fall landscape is made up in most part by the late-blooming Asters and Chrysanthemums, and it is from these that we can extend our seasonal color.

Among the carry-overs are Abelias. To think that we heralded its flowering in mid-June and it is still in production, prettier than ever as it now carries ripening seed pods as well as flowers. This, too, is true of Gordonia lasianthus, another evergreen of the highest standards. In a small and limited garden space they are the types that count. I must mention Althaea Diane, the newest of the pure white variety and a consistent bloomer.

For myself, however, I can forget all plants other than Camellias since this is the best month for the fall bloomers, both the Sasanqua and Japonica species. Zone 8 can rightfully be called the Camellia belt of this country and there should not be a single home in our area that does not boast of at least one plant. You will find in our Camellia section varieties that naturally bloom in the fall, and with careful selection you can have Camellias with slight interruptions until spring.

The Grounsel Bush, Baccharis halimifolia, which frequents our salt marshes along the eastern seacoast, is possibly the most spectacular shrub at this time of the year, as it readies to sow its seed heads following a short and inconspicuous blooming period. These white powder-puff-like capsules smother the plant and give it the appearance of being wrapped up in foam. They are seldom seen or offered in commerce. Therefore, inland gardens are deprived of this October beauty, although it will thrive on high land away from its natural habitat. They grow to ten feet if permitted, but can be maintained to any size through pruning.

Up until now the Alexandrian Laurel, *Danae racemosa,* sometimes called Poets Laurel, has been an attractive but unobtrusive evergreen in our shade gardens. At this time, however, its marble-sized berries turn a cherry red and are evenly distributed along graceful stems made up of small foliage. The common name, Poets Laurel, comes from the practice in ancient Greece of decorating the brows of the illustrious bards with these berried stems. If nothing else the yard-long arching branches give them a mark of distinction, and make them interesting as a ground cover under taller shrubs or trees.

A perfect companion plant to Camellias and Azaleas, Poets Laurel grows to two feet before arching over. They are most useful as cut flower material in arrangements, and are so used in the trade. While considered in most garden encyclopedias as a tender sub-tropical, they will tolerate our Zone 8 and should be sought. Being a native of the rich portions of the Near East, Syria and Persia, they prefer their portion of the soil to be well impregnated with bone meal or at least I have found it so in my own garden, where they have greatly multiplied from underground divisions. Poets Laurel is a conversation piece at any time of the year, especially now, if you can lure the birds away from them. The berries are

also a source of seed.

Many areas of our growing zone do not realize that Jerusalem cherries, *Solanun pseudo capsicum,* can be grown out of doors as a hardy annual, persisting with its colorful berries until the turn of the year. In many instances they reseed themselves year after year, acting somewhat as a perennial. If you have never tried them as such, buy a package of Christmas Cherry Jubilee, whose whitish berries change to orange before the holidays. The entire plant stands the early frosty nights, and will thrive in either full sun or partial shade.

October Work Schedule

It is very important, as winter becomes a closer reality, to learn your area's growing days. This information is in the front of the book and is an indication of when an area will have its first frost—and how long a gardener should be active into November.

These are variations in growing days due to altitude and location, and they are noted here to remind us that they have a tendency to regulate our work schedule. It is possible that in your own area the fluctuation may be even greater in lesser distances than it is in Virginia. As strange as it seems, Williamsburg, less than thirty-five miles from Norfolk, has only 194 growing days compared to Norfolk's 254 and Richmond's 220. Yet Atlanta, five hundred miles south of Norfolk and one thousand feet higher above sea level, is closer in climate with 233 growing days.

These figures relating to temperatures should be noted at this time of the year, for they reveal that October, with its cooler nights and days and frost-free predictions on average, is the best planting month, in spite of our wide climate variations even in such a limited area as Zone 8.

I consider fall planting, or transplanting, much more productive than that done in the spring if but for one reason, that the disturbed roots of the plants have a much longer period to readjust themselves before actual top growth resumes. Within this temperate zone, where frost penetration is minimal and soil temperatures at a foot below ground level may average fifty degrees, roots remain active. Since the shock of moving plants is for the most part due to the loss of part of their root system, this condition is a plus.

Nevertheless, transplanted plants will need much more top pruning to re-establish their root balance than nursery grown plants, which are normally prepared for the shock through proper pruning of the root-system as well as their top growth. While on this subject, an analysis of container grown plants' reaction to transplanting is in order, since we tend to minimize the fact that they too suffer shock, although from a different source.

Container grown plants are constantly force fed nutrients and water to compensate for their lack of proper space and soil. Consequently, roots have not been allowed to grow as nature intended, but were forced into spirals, and survived only because they were consistently attended. Therefore my recommendation in the handling of a container grown plant is to take the plant out of the container and dip it in a bucket of water, to which a solution of a commercial transplanting mixture has been added until it can no longer absorb

any. In examining the ball, if it appears very container bound, loosen it before planting, so that the tiny roots will have a chance to spread. If such an operation is necessary it must be done very gently through rolling the ball on the ground with some slight pressure; then proceed to plant it and water it in with the remains of the transplanting solution and additional solution if needed.

Any planting should be preceeded by adequate preparation of the area, whether it entails the planting of a perennial bed or a single shrub. We must remind ourselves that this initial operation can only be done on one occasion, as we will never again have the opportunity to place the nutrients where they belong to encourage the roots to penetrate into the subsoil. It is a fact that even the most active of chemical fertilizers will not move over six inches beyond its initial location in any direction.

Plants considered to be of a permanent nature, such as most shrubs and especially trees, should be planted with this in mind. Take the case of Lilacs, which originated in limestone country. The time to supply them their necessary diet by adding plenty of limestone to the subsoil is when you are excavating the planting pocket. In our part of the country, where oyster shells

deploy roots before planting

Transplanting from containers.

are plentiful, we use them for drainage and as a source of calcium. Ground limestone or Dolemetic lime will do. You might also save bones from your garbage to incorporate into the subsoil for those plants that need it. But none of this material will do much good if not placed deep enough to reach the root systems.

The size of the planting holes will of course be entirely predicated on what you are planting. For example, an ordinary Rose bush should be set in no less than an eighteen inch square or round hole. Most experienced gardeners believe that a square hole is better than a round one, to keep roots from spiralling. These remarks may sound unimportant in this day when we believe so much in scientific formulas, but I wonder if nature has really changed so much with all our advancements in horticulture.

November

The greatest challenge of gardening within Zone 8 comes at this time when most indexes point to wrapping up the garden for the winter. Evidence of Winter's approach abounds since most of our native plants have been frost-bitten and deciduous foliage is covering the hardened ground. Therefore we must search from among the unusual for a November performer, and my favorite at this time is the Strawberry Tree, *Arbutus unedo*. It is just coming into bloom with its white Lily-of-the-Valley-like flowers hanging in terminal clusters on a bush reaching fifteen to

Strawberry Tree, *Arbutus unedo,* a favorite of mine.
Inset from National Arboretum photo.

eighteen feet. In its maturity the limbs become twisted, giving it a picturesque form with its main trunks scaling as its brown bark takes on a reddish hue.

This native of southern Europe, introduced in southern California during the last century, finally caught our attention and is offered in limited quantities in southern nurseries. It is perfectly hardy to our zone and maintains its evergreen foliage, which turns a rusty bronze after the winter freezes. Its delicate flower clusters will keep on opening until after the turn of the year, and then set fruit not unlike Strawberries, from which it gets its name. They must taste good to the birds who devour them even before they thoroughly ripen. *Arbutus* belong to the Heath family, so that the common Heather makes a good companion plant, especially those blooming during the same period such as Springwood Pink and its counterpart, the white variety. It is hard to picture a better combination at this time of the year unless we turn to the many Camellias which also abound.

November is the time members of the Sasanqua species perform best, of which I shall describe six which I consider most suitable for landscape use. A list of favorites would be headed by the most floriferous Papaver, in bloom since October with large single cup-form soft pink blossoms. In that same category would be Sparkling Burgundy, an American variety of unusual form with ruby-rose double flowers overlaid with a sheen of lavender. Pink Princess, with deep rose-pink semi-double flowers, is probably a chance seedling from Mine-No-Yuki, an older variety from Japan, whose translated name means snow on the peak, indicating flowers of the purest white. Both are eye stoppers in the fall landscape. The two final performers for the November landscape are the Japanese varieties Hinode-Gumo, meaning Dawn Cloud, and Hiodoshi, Scarlet-Threaded Suit. Both have large single flowers with the first being a pale white to pink and the latter a crimson splashed with white.

No November landscape should be without a Loquat, *Eriobotrya japonica*, a small tree, which grows from twelve to fifteen feet tall. Its evergreen foliage is a show unto itself with leaves up to twelve inches long and half as broad. Green above and brown beneath, the leaves are deeply veined in red. At this time of the year it has panicles of white flowers that will send you searching for its elusive fragrance. What a find for Thanksgiving decorations.

I must warn you that in the colder areas of Zone 8 it will need the protection of a courtyard or a wall with a southern exposure. Its flexible limb structure permits espaliering which is a most effective use for this leathery evergreen. Its foliage and fragrance, so long lasting in flower arrangements, dictate the Loquat's use in our gardens. Other outstanding plants that add a touch of the tropical to protected areas are the *Eucalyptus gunni* and the Windmill Palm, *Trachycarpus*, both known to have survived zero temperatures for short lapses of time.

While the common Wax-Myrtle, *Myrica carolinensis*, also known as Bayberry, is recognized by most everyone, it is one of our most useful evergreen shrubs, adaptable to most situations, from swampy lands to high, arid locations. It was at this time of the year that early settlers gathered its

Loquat.

berries for the processing of wax and the manufacture of candles. This aromatic shrub should find a use in any garden as time has not dimmed its beauty.

During November, most of us at some time or other have encountered Persimmons in our travels through open pastures or thin woodlands. Its colorful fruit is delicious if sufficiently frost-bitten. The native *Diospyros virginiana* makes up into a beautiful tree of around fifty feet especially attractive at this time of the year with its autumn foliage.

I also wish to call your attention to the Oriental species, *Diospyros kaki*, handled by many southern nurseries. This Persimmon produces fruit the size of an Apple which ripens at this time and turns the color of an orange, a magnificent sight hanging against its green foliage. Besides its sweet tasty fruit, this species makes up into a wonderful ornamental tree growing to only

Persimmon Tree *Diospyros virginiana.* National Arboretum photo.

fifteen feet. They are both best planted in pairs for better pollination.

November Work Schedule

By this time, we should have our planting and replanting schedule fairly well organized, with most of the perennials cut back except for the late blooming Mums and fall Asters. Be sure to label these for spring divisions if the need be. If you have not planted all of your spring bulbs, there is still ample time.

I would like to give you my formula for bulb planting, should it fit your program. Tulips, for instance, which at best flower three successive years, should be planted at least eight inches deep, normally a couple of inches deeper than recommended. I believe this added depth adds another year to their florescence, provided their planting pocket has been excavated to a foot deep, with some well-rotted humus or native peat moss worked into the subsoil to which has been added a liberal sprinkling of bone meal to attract their root system to that depth and keep them cool in summer.

German Iris Snow Drop Grape Hyacinth Crocus Bulbous Iris Madonna Lily (base rooting) *Alliums saillias* Hyacinth other Lilies (Stem rooting) Daffodil Tulip

Bulbs

Individual planting pockets dug a foot square and deep will accommodate up to eight individual bulbs, with space available to incorporate other plants for a transition of color. As noted in the June work schedule, some of the easier to germinate annual seeds can be dropped among these ripening bulbs, affording a more interesting garden. Under this system, spring bulbs are planted to incorporate color until other perennials take over. For it will not be too long before the established *Triteleia uniflora* will carpet the ground with their delightful violet blue flowers in company with the early yellow Crocus.

Planting time means having an ample supply of organic materials to incorporate in the soil. I have never seen soil so poor, whether of sandy or clay composition, that it could not be rejuvenated with humus of some sort, because its bacterial contents will reactivate any soil. I normally reserve my chemical fertilizers for spring and summer use. Fall planting is benefited more by incorporating organic fertilizers, such as bone meal, cottonseed meal, bloodmeal, and fertilizers derived from fish and the droppings of the stockyards.

Mulching materials are important to incorporate at this time, especially to protect newly planted materials. It is amazing the many kinds of mulches that are available, more or less predicated on their economic production in various areas. Anything that is organic and can be shredded economically will insulate the soil surface, such as peanut shells or corn husks or other crop surplus which was once wasted. Mulches extracted from wood pulp or evergreen needles are still most popular. Few of the mountains of sawdust

that once dotted the landscape are still available, as they, too, have been processed into valuable mulch.

In your fall planting you should incorporate some new plant that did not grow there before, and perhaps from our time table section you have been able to select at least one. We have presented them in their seasonal sequence to help you fill in some particular time in which your garden may be the weakest.

December

The last month in the calendar year brings pleasure to our lives through the silhouettes of bare limbs in contrast to the texture of evergreen foliage, the playing of lights and shadows, the fascination of berried branches, and the animation created by the birds in their quest for survival. This winter landscape is all the more fascinating when viewed through a picture window as we settle in front of a warm fire with good company.

Perhaps my attempt to create such a scene may serve as a guideline for your garden and through using your own imagination and existing props you, too, can create a winter wonderland. There are dozens of ways to accomplish the same objective—enjoying the next three inclement months inside, looking out.

When I bought my lot I had a lovely Hackberry, *Celtis laevigata*, growing about twenty feet north of where our house would be sitting. In fact this deciduous tree with its cork-like bark was one of the main reasons we built the house there. It overlooked a ravine in which grew twisted clumps of native Hollies, *Ilex opaca*, twisted from their struggle to get a share of the sunlight.

This Hackberry became the focal point for planning our terrace, which is flagstone separated by *Mondo,* fanning out like a spider's web. To anchor the base of the Hackberry to the ground, Japanese Spurge, *Pachysandra terminalis,* was planted in a four foot diameter circle to blend with the *Mondo.* Both are evergreen, do not grow over four inches tall, and can stand the root competition of the tree, drought, and shade, when well established.

I then proceeded to plant one of my favorite Camellias, Dawn, of the species *Vernalis,* as another focal point. It will bloom from December to March and is only interrupted in its progress when the temperature falls below twenty-five degrees, to resume when it goes above freezing. Falling temperatures force careful selectivity of planting material when dealing with the winter landscape. A few yards away is another Camellia, Shishi-Gashira, of the *Hiemalis* species. It too has a special purpose, blooming from Thanksgiving to New Year's in a dwarf form. Many variations of these plants can be incorporated, but my two give me lively color on the bleakest days.

A bird feeder is hung on my Hollies over a birdbath to lure those nibblers away from the glistening berries, and believe me it works. You can take it

Looking out my picture window.

from there to attain any desired goal. Let's discuss some of the plants that could serve an identical purpose, for had not the American Holly been there I might have planted the Youpon, another of the American species, because it does not play host to the Holly Leaf Miner, nor any other pest that I can think of. It also colors up earlier and is overlooked by most birds.

Perhaps I would have planted a Clump-Birch instead of the Hackberry because it is typical of the snow-country, and its catkins and peeling bark are so attractive in the winter landscape. Texture is a most important factor when most of the deciduous trees are bare.

We don't expect much flower color at this season, which is the reason berried shrubs are important. In the Holly family I favor the Lusterleaf, *Ilex latifolia,* because it looks like an evergreen Magnolia, with the extra quality of berry clusters. Some of the hybrid Hollies are also superior to the straight species such as the Burford, *Cornuta burfordi,* and Nellie Stevens, *Aquifolium.* The time to pick Hollies and for that matter any other berried shrub, is during the winter, when they are at their best.

One of the most unusual performers at this season is the tropical looking Fatsia, *Aralia sieboldi.* Normally offered in the trade as a houseplant or greenhouse specimen, this plant has survived fifteen years in my garden. Its large glossy evergreen foliage resembles that of a Castor Bean plant and produces umbels of white flowers at this time of the year. As seen from our picture window on a winter's day, it has prompted my wife, Florrie, to call it our thermometer plant because if the

temperature falls below thirty degrees the umbels droop, soon straightening out when it rises above freezing.

This year I became interested in the Chinese Gooseberry, *Actinidia arguta,* sometimes sold as Kiwi Fruit, or Tara Vine, primarily because they are under scrutiny at our local experimental station. Native of China and northern India, this vine, which grows to forty feet with fabulous rapidity in this area, will take over and attach itself to nearby trees. You must have at least one male vine if you wish to harvest the greenish-yellow fruits which are about the size of Gooseberries, and, incidentally, taste quite like them. I am sure your local experimental station can tell you all about this plant and how to treat it. I understand that it is much sought after by gourmet markets.

If you are not acquainted with the Jujube Date Tree, you might want to try one; it makes up into a beautiful ornamental which while in leaf looks like it might be an evergreen, but it is not. It too originates from China and India, and is possibly the hardiest of the fruits. While there are several species listed under the genus *Zizyphus,* the Chinese species is the hardiest one. They thrive in alkaline soil, so should be afforded a lot of lime in planting and thereafter.

Walking through my own garden at year's end I meditated on the cast that had given me so much pleasure and how early winter had come to pull down the final curtain. There was a skim of snow on the ground mixed with frost, and as I neared the end of a shaded path, something drew my attention. I had not remembered planting some corms of a hardy Cyclamen,

Cyclamen neapolitanum, but there, on this dismal New Year's Eve, they had peaked through, seemingly to wish me a happy New Year.

There are many species of Hardy Cyclamen, with all having typical Cyclamen foliage in miniature. This one has lilac-pink flowers about an inch high; others as C. europaeum, cilicum africanum bloom throughout the summer, but of course with much more competition from the outside world. The entire tribe are quite unpredictable in their blooming schedule or for that matter the appearance of their mottled foliage above ground. They relish a deep cool woodsy soil in a shaded nook, and can often be pur-

chased from bulb specialists who carry unusual plants.

My intention was to introduce you to some of the plants that have become my favorites over the years, to tell you how and why they add such pleasure to my garden. Nurseries and catalogs will present you with many more varieties and species, and my hope is that you will view each new addition to your garden not only for its peak performance, but for its idiosyncracies, its silhouette in the landscape, and, perhaps most important, its year-round performance.

No month is better than December, with Christmas in the air to remember that gardening is not just a springtime

Fatsia.

thing. We should strive to be more than fair weather friends to our gardens, which afford us unique beauty and pleasure every month of the year.

December Work Schedule

By now frost has taken its toll on most of the deciduous vegetation. A new year is soon to begin and it is time to decide which chores should be done first to prepare our gardens.

As I sharpen my shears and pruning tools for the main job ahead I am saddened by seeing the last Rose proudly holding up its withered blossom. It is a reminder that the imminent wintry blasts may loosen its root system if too much of the limb structure is left exposed to the elements. Therefore, like most good Rosarians, I cut back about half of the current year's growth. Of course, this is not considered their main pruning, which will be left until March.

The most important work schedule for December is to make certain that all transplanted shrubs and trees have been well anchored with stakes and guide wires, if needed, so that their root systems can re-establish themselves. A rocking tree or bush will not be afforded that opportunity.

Perhaps last but not least, make sure nothing has been too deeply planted, a condition which I believe causes more than fifty percent of all casualties. With that in mind we can enjoy the holidays as we browse and study all of the new catalogs that come to us before and after the New Year.

Well-anchored tree to allow disturbed
root system to re-anchor itself.

Annuals

It has been said that the best way to entice people to become gardeners is to give them a package of annual seeds, which will germinate within a week and in thirty days be in bloom. To be part of this metamorphosis is indeed a thrill.

While all annuals do not respond so well to our touch, they nevertheless are among the easiest of plants to cultivate, provided we choose those most adaptable to our climatic conditions and place them in an environment best suited to their well being. With thousands of them listed in seed catalogs which cater to the national scene, I have dared to pick forty species which I believe will best suit Zone 8 with a few varieties in each that are proven performers.

While most annuals will bloom within ninety days after sowing and have spent themselves during the same period, picking off the dead blooms will considerably lengthen that time. Annuals coming to us from all portions of the earth are individualistic in their needs, some preferring shade, others full sunlight. Many originate from desert countries, others from lush plains and deep woodlands.

Plant hybridists have performed wonders in making available to the average gardeners colors, vigor, and adaptability that only a few years ago were thought impossible. We also have the All-America trial grounds where annuals are being tested under various climatic conditions. Many of these are F1 hybrids, which indicates that they are inter-crossed but unable to reproduce their true characteristics unless put through the original process of cross-breeding. Therefore it is imperative for favorable results with annuals, to start off with a good source of seed.

In this presentation you will note that for each species we indicate the number of seeds per ounce. This information is necessary because it predicates the proper manner in which the seeds are to be sown.

Seed packets will average fifty seeds, unless otherwise specified, which is ample for the average home gardener. However, some species such as Begonias produce two million seeds per ounce, whereas others such as Zinnias only three thousand. In handling seeds which are as microscopic as Begonias, extra care must be taken. In fact, I recommend that you buy Begonia plants whose seed-count is over sixty thousand as seedlings because they are so difficult to germinate under ordinary home conditions.

Impatiens and Petunias, which have 285 thousand seeds per ounce, and other finer seeds are available in seed tapes with the seeds evenly spaced in a transparent paraffin-like substance which readily disintegrates in contact with moisture. These are normally available in fifteen foot tapes with the seeds one-half inch apart, and they are well worth the extra cost. Unfortunately, this is a recent method and not all seeds are available in tapes.

Sowing in seed flats.
First Phase—sowing of seeds at random
Second Phase—Transplanting in rows

Tiny seeds which are not offered as seed tapes are best handled by emptying and thoroughly incorporating the contents of one packet in a cup of dry sand, then evenly distributing the mixture in a seed flat. Press it into a smooth surface and sprinkle lightly with water to settle the seed in place. Cover the area with a sheet of cellophane or glass, then a sheet of newsprint to keep them in darkness until germinated. If the soil moisture has been well dampened before the operation they will not need added moisture until exposed to the light. Granulated sphagnum moss is an even better medium for sowing fine seeds such as Begonias. Watering, as needed, should be done with an atomizer until the seedlings are large enough to transplant. There are also various seed starter kits offered on the market which will greatly help in giving annuals a start.

Annuals are a bright source of color and variety for your Summer garden. The spent blossoms need to be constantly pinched off, and the plants require adequate moisture. Fertilizer should only be used if vigorous growth is lacking since it not only fails to correct problems at times, but under certain circumstances can actually create stress. However, it is easy enough to meet the annuals' requirements, and the pleasure they bring is well worth the effort.

Forty Annuals

1. **Ageratum** (200,000 seeds per ounce). They can be sown in March under cover to flower in May, June, and July. For a continual display, another sowing in June would flower from August until frost. Due to the minute size of the seed it is best for the average gardener to purchase the plants as seedlings, ready to set out. Ageratum grows to five or six inches tall and spreads a foot or more. Suggested varieties are Royal or Blue Blazer, Blue Mink, or a white variety, Summer Snow.

Ageratum.

2. **Sweet Alyssum** (90,000 seeds per ounce). It is best sown directly where it is to grow or in peat pots for later transplanting. It blooms in May, June, and on into the summer with occasional grooming necessary to keep seed pods from forming. Sweet Alys-

sum is ideal as a border plant for it grows three inches high and spreads. Recommended varieties are the white Tiny Tim or Carpet of Snow, Royal Carpet, a new hybrid of violet or purple, and Pastel Carpet, a mixture of rose, dark violet, pink, white, and cream yellow.

3. **Amaranthus** (7,000 seeds per ounce). It is a tall growing annual to four feet. Sow it directly where it is wanted or in peat pots for later transplanting. Recommended varieties are Flaming Fountain, Tricolor Perfection, and Early Splendor.

4. **Asters** (12,000 seeds per ounce). They prefer cool weather for better performance so sow them indoors in March to flower in May or June, or sow them outdoors in June to flower from September until frost. Careful watering is necessary to insure consistent moisture, never too wet or too dry. Many varieties and colors are offered. Be sure to select from wilt-resistant strains and dwarf types which are best suited for home gardens. One particularly good variety is Pepite Mixture in red, white, and blue.

5. **Begonias** (2,000,000 seeds per ounce). This is the Semperflorens type and is better purchased as a flowering plant ready to set out in May. May varieties will be offered at your favorite garden shop, providing the color combination best for your garden. If you wish to grow your own, sow seeds in January in a sterilized starting mixture in temperatures around sixty degrees. Within a month they will be ready to pinch back and they can be held in small peat pots or transferred to four-inch pots planting out in early May. Begonias are best grown in semi-shade to full shade. There are dwarf varieties

Begonias.

of five inches such as Viva, a snow-white, and Thousand Wonders, a bright pink. The Butterfly Series can be had in red, pink, and white. This one grows to ten or twelve inches. Do not over-fertilize them once planted in rich, peaty soil. They will bloom consistently until frost and are one of the best annuals for shaded areas, although they will tolerate full sun if kept adequately watered.

6. **Balsam** (3,300 seeds per ounce). This is an old-fashioned annual which belongs to the same family as Impatiens, preferring a semi-shade to shade exposure. Seed should be sown in the open ground in early May and thinned to be ten to twelve inches apart. As with Impatiens, it prefers a peaty loam. The extra-dwarf, double-flowering varieties such as Tom Thumb Scarlet and Tom Thumb White, are preferable for the small garden. There is also a variety called Torch, which is bright red. They generally will start flowering within sixty days and continue through frost. Once established in the garden, they will repeat from seed thereafter.

The most similar blue flower that will also thrive in the shade would be Torenia.

7. Browallia (180,000 seeds per ounce). A good annual for window boxes and hanging baskets, it is best sown in March indoors. Plant it outdoors in May. It prefers semi-shade. One recommended variety is Sapphire, which grows ten inches and features dark blue flowers with a dark eye. Powder Blue and Silver Bells are a snowy white and bloom consistently until frost, and if grown in containers can be brought in for winter blooming.

Silver Bells, *Browallia.*

8. Candytuft (9,500 seeds per ounce). Perhaps one of the easiest annuals to grow, it can be sown in place where it will flower any time after April 15. While it is normally thought of as a white border plant, such as the new Super Iceberg, there is a new clone called Red Flash. It will flower within sixty days, but make another sowing in mid-June for a continuous carpet. It is one of the plants you can use as a ground cover, with taller and more erect plants interspersed for contrast. It grows to ten or twelve inches tall and broad.

9. Castor Bean, *Ricinus* (25 to 57 seeds per ounce). For anyone wishing a spectacular, tall plant, growing from five to eight feet with tropical-like foliage which turns deep crimson, this is it. The flowers themselves are inconspicuous. Only a few seeds need be planted after mid-April and placed four to six feet apart. It creates an unusual background or hedge.

10. Chrysanthemum (9,000 seeds per ounce). While Mums are normally treated as perennials, many can be treated as annuals by sowing the seed indoors in March and transplanting into peat pots to be set outdoors in early May. They will flower from September through November. When such F1 hybrids as Autumn Glory and Korean Sunset Mixed are used they will start flowering in August. These types grow only a foot, but will make up to eighteen inch plants with one and one-half to two inch flowers, in colors ranging from white to deep autumn colors.

11. Cockscomb, *Celosia* (40,000 seeds per ounce). They are easy to raise and can be sown outdoors after mid-April. They will color within ninety days and continue until frost under clean cultivation. They prefer full sun and can be dried under special treatment for indoor arrangements. There are many forms available, such as the new superdwarf, which grows only ten inches high, with combs as wide. The recommended varieties are Empress, crimson red, Red Fox, a crimson plumed type over twenty-four inches, and Golden Feather, also a plumed variety.

12. **Coleus** (100,000 seeds per ounce). This is fast becoming the most popular bedding plant because of its neat and brilliant foliage coloring, which remains so from the time it is planted out permanently in early May until cut down by frost. Sow it under protection in March and transplant it to peat pots once germinated. It is a warm-temperature plant. The so-called Rainbow, a fringed-leaved mixture, is one of the best, although it can be had in separate named blends.

13. **Cosmos** (2,500 seeds per ounce). They are best planted to flower in the cooler months of October by sowing the seeds outdoors in late August. The variety Diabolo, a brillant red, is exceptionally good for our warm area and will bloom in two months from seed. Bright Lights is also a good mixture, producing red, orange, and yellow shades.

14. **Crapemyrtle** (5,000 seeds per ounce). Annual hybrids can be sown in February and march indoors, and individual seedlings transferred to three inch peat pots to be set outdoors permanently in May to flower in July and August. These dwarf clones grow from eighteen to twenty-four inch plants and repeat year after year.

15. **Dahlias** (2,800 seeds per ounce). These are among our most consistent bloomers, flowering from June until frost. Sow them indoors in February or March and transfer them to three inch peat pots to set outside in May. The dwarf types, which grow to eighteen inches with individual four-inch flowers, are best suited for flower

beds. Set them eighteen to twenty-four inches apart. One of the newer varieties, Redskin, with glossy bronze foliage, produces double flowers with a wide range of rich colors. There are many other strains.

Dianthus deltoides Zing.

16. **Dianthus** (25,000 seeds per ounce). While considered a perennial, the newer varieties of Dianthus such as Queen of Hearts, will bloom, beginning in June, continuously into early winter, with multitudes of cardinal red clusters of flowers. If the flowers are removed when spent, the plant will never stop blooming. Sow the seeds indoors in March and set out in late April. It grows from twelve to fifteen inches high and can be set one foot apart for mass effects. For a truly red flower, this is a must. There are other colors available such as Merry-Go-Round, a pure white with the same growing habit.

17. **Exacum** (1,000,000 seeds per ounce). Because these are minute seeds, the best method is to mix a package, which may have as many as 500 seeds, with a spoonful of sand to facilitate their distribution. Then sow them in individual two to two and one-half inch pots filled with a prepared soil mixture and just press into the surface any time in March and April. Set them out six to eight inches apart in beds, planter boxes, or hanging baskets. Varieties suggested are Affine, which grows to be a twelve inch compact plant, and Blythe Spirit, a variety that is white, grows to eight inches, and is an exclusive of Park Seeds.

18. **Gaillardia** (14,000 seeds per ounce). The annual species normally sold under the name of Lollipop is a compact-growing variety that grows to ten inches and blooms all summer from seeds or seedlings set outdoors after April 15. This mixture comes in red, butterscotch bronze, and lemon colors. It will stand dry locations in full sun. Do not confuse it with the perennial species.

19. **Gazania** (12,000 seeds per ounce). This is another dry and heat-resisting annual. It can be sown where it is to bloom after April 15. Fire Emerald is perhaps the easiest variety to germinate and will bloom a couple of months from sowing, producing three and one-half inch flowers on twelve to fifteen inch plants in a great pastel range of colors, including yellows and bronzes.

20. **Geraniums,** *Pelargonium* (6,000 seeds per ounce). Geraniums will be offered by the trade in many different types and colors. However, the new Carefree varieties can be started in February or March, set out in mid-April in three-inch pots to flower outdoors all summer. They are available in separate colors—scarlet, rose, pink, and white.

21. **Heliotrope** (52,500 seeds per ounce). It requires twenty-five days to germinate and is well worth growing for its wonderful fragrance. Regal Dwarf is the easiest to grow. As it is a cool-loving annual, it should be sown in peat pots outdoors in June for fall flowering. It comes in various tones of blue-lavender and grows to fifteen inches.

22. **Impatiens** (60,000 seeds per ounce). Many varieties and types of these will be offered by the trade in time to set out in early May for flowering all summer until frost. They are the best for shady gardens; in fact, they resent full sun. The varieties are many. Perhaps one of the best is called Shady Lady, which produces white to deep reds and many pastel shades. Excellent for planter boxes and hanging baskets, they can be brought in before frost to continue blooming indoors.

23. **Larkspur** (8,000 seeds per ounce). This stately annual should be sown in September or October to produce its three to four foot spikes of flowers the following June or July. Because it resents transplanting, it is best to sow two or three seeds in a three inch peat pot, later thin it out to a single plant and set out in October, or, of course, sow it out permanently. It requires from twenty to twenty-five days to germinate and is best covered with damp burlap until then. The plants will go through winter as an evergreen tuft and should not be over-mulched, as they are apt to rot out before spring. Just a light covering of Pine straw will carry them over. The so-called Imperial Giants grow four to

five feet tall and can be had in blue, dark blue, scarlet, pink, and white. They are best kept staked as they develop their flower spikes. There is a new blend, Dwarf Hyacinth, but it has not been sufficiently tested in this area. For superior performance start fertilizing only after the flower buds appear on the stalks.

24. **Lobelia,** *Erinus* (750,000 seeds per ounce). Crystal Palace Compacta or Blue Cascade are possibly the best blue flowers in the floral kingdom, but not the easiest to produce. They are advocated for window or planter boxes or hanging baskets lined with sphagnum moss, so that their tiny root systems can be kept cool. Do not grow them where extreme heat will get to them. They prefer semi-shade like that found under the filtered light of tall Pines. Refer to Exacum for their cultivation.

Hybrid Yellow Nugget Marigolds.
Burpee Seeds Photo.

25. **Marigolds** (9,000 seeds per ounce). They hardly need explanation, except to note that you select varieties for either cut-flower use or for bedding. The dwarf types are most desirable, such as the Double French which grows to twelve inches. Sow directly outdoors in mid-April, preferably in full sun,to

take over where early flowering bulbs are planted, or as colorful border plants. Other recommended dwarf varieties are Bolero, Golden Boy, and Gold Nugget.

26. **Morning Glory,** *Ipomoea* (650 seeds per ounce). In 1976, through Japanese hybridists, this well-known vine became available in red, white, and blue under the name of Japanese Imperial Strain. They are best sown in individual three inch peat pots after mid-April, and permanently planted outdoors within a month. They are most accommodating to culture and look lovely when climbing a trellis or encircling a small tree, such as a Crapemyrtle.

27. **Nicotania** (50,000 seeds per ounce). This has become one of the most adaptable annuals in recent years, due to hybridization. It will flower consistently from June until frost from seeds sown indoors in March. They are best germinated in peat pots and not disturbed until planted out, preferably in full sun. There are dwarf types, such as Idol, a new dwarf red flower that grows less than one inch tall, Dwarf White Bedder, and one of the most attractive, Lime Sherbet, an entirely new color. All are deliciously fragrant.

28. **Ornamental Peppers** *Capsicum* (10,000 seeds per ounce). They are relatively new for our gardens, producing Ornamental Peppers whose colorings are most intriguing. Good varieties are Black Prince, which bears black candle-like fruit that changes to bright red in the autumn. Fiesta has two-inch bell-shaped white fruit that turns bright red. All of these grow ten to twelve inches high and are best started in peat pots in mid-April. They do best in full sun.

Pansies.

29. Pansies (20,000 seeds per ounce). They should prove to be our first show of color in the spring, as during mild winters they will start blooming after the turn of the year and normally persist until July. Because they are not so easy to germinate it is best to purchase them as flowering plants, normally available in late winter and early spring, unless you wish to sow them indoors before November. The varieties are numerous, normally classified as Swiss Giants, and obtainable either mixed or in separate colors such as blue, yellow, orange, red, rose, or combinations. They are invaluable for planters, window boxes, and hanging baskets and also as ground cover plants with Tulips and early-flowering bulbs.

30. Petunias (285,000 seeds per ounce). Petunias require no introduction and are being offered in many colors in single and double flowers and in upright or cascading varieties. They

meet all requirements for bedding or border planting, for hanging baskets and window boxes, and for any use your imagination can devise.

They are not foolproof, however, and will require attention in watering and keeping all spent blooms from setting seed. May planting, as well as another August planting, will be best for continuity.

31. Portulaca (280,000 seeds per ounce). This annual is not the best known, although it has a very important use as a border plant along hot-dry conditions, such as a gravel driveway. The seeds are very tiny, and therefore an average packet with a couple of hundred seeds should be mixed in a quart of dry sand and lightly sprinkled in place, as they do not stand transplanting, or, of course, they can be started in small peat pots. Some of the newer strains are most spectacular, such as the Tuffet strain, which is available in golden, scarlet, yellow, or mixed. They will germinate in ten days when sown in May and bloom in sixty days. Each plant grows about six inches high and as broad and blooms only during the day.

32. Salvia (7,500 seeds per ounce). The so-called Spendens are no doubt the most consistent bloomers and are now available in dwarf varieties such as St. John's Fire, Flamenco in deep red, and Snow Tips in white. They grow twelve inches tall, but there are also medium and tall-growing varieties. If sown in March indoors and set out in May, they will bloom consistently from June until frost.

33. Salvia Farinacea (23,500 seeds per ounce). This perennial Salvia can be treated as an annual and if sown at the same time as other annuals, Bonfire types will bloom just as quickly and long. They are included because the new varieties of Blue Bedder, Blue Spike, and Catima add a new dimension in blues which are rather scarce in the flower world. They grow from twenty-four to thirty-six inches high on strong, stiff stems.

34. **Snapdragon,** *Antirrhinum* (180,000 seeds per ounce). They have been bred to stand our summer heat. If selected from dwarf varieties such as Floral Carpet they will require no staking and bloom consistently outdoors from June to freezing by keeping the spent blooms eliminated. Their colors range from bronze, pink, red, rose, orchid, white, and yellow. They can be sown in March for June flowering, or in June for a new fall crop. There is also the Rocket series and Bright Butterflies, which grow to thirty-six inches for cut-flower purposes. Snapdragons resist the cold. Once established, they will repeat year after year, if planted in a well-protected sunny area.

35. **Spider Plant** (15,000 seeds per ounce). They are good bedding plants for a background effect, growing from three to four feet. Normally, once established in a garden, they will repeat from self-sown seeds year after year. They can be sown outdoors in early April to flower in July. Separate colors can be had in pink, rose, and white, such as Pink Queen, Cherry Queen, and Helen Campbell Snow Crown.

36. **Strawflower,** *Helichrysum,* (36,000 seeds per ounce). This is one of the best annuals for dried winter bouquets. The variety Monstrosum grows to thirty inches and produces double flowers in red, purple, rose, salmon, yellow, white, or a mixture of these. The exposure of the seeds to light is essential to germination so do not cover them with soil. They can be sown directly where they are to blossom for late summer harvesting or earlier indoors for late spring flowering.

37. **Torenia** (375,000 seeds per ounce). These tenacious little annuals sometimes called the Wishbone Flower are not sufficiently known in this area; they provide a continuous flow of small flowers from July until frost. Seeds can be started indoors or sown outdoors in April. Because the seeds are tiny, mix them in a cupful of dry sand for easier distribution. They germinate in fifteen days and flower in sixty. Their overall height is twelve inches and they are covered with tiny, Pansy-like flowers in either blue or white. The varieties Fournieri Nana Compacta Blue and Fournieri Nana Compacta White are the principal strains. They are invaluable in borders and window or planter boxes as well as hanging baskets, and can be transferred indoors for winter flowering. They tolerate full sun, but are happier in filtered sunlight.

38. **Verbena** (10,000 seeds per ounce). Fortunately, hybridists have given us new strains of this valuable annual. Among the latest is the Spirit of '76, a mixture of red, white, and blue flowers which grows to eight inches high, and eventually spreads to make a solid ground cover. Sow them in March to flower in June, or later outdoors for later flowering, which they will consistently do until frost. They prefer full sun. Verbena Venosa is a hardy perennial which produces lavender flowers and is one of our ground covers, but can be treated like the annual species. Verbena is one of the best plants to use for hanging baskets or wherever a trailing plant is needed.

39. Vinca Rosea (21,000 seeds per ounce). Sometimes called the Creeping Periwinkle, this is one of the easiest annuals to grow from seeds sown in March and transplanted outside in May. These dwarf to six inch plants will bloom consistently until frost and stand either sun or shade. The new Polka Dot variety has sparkling waxy foliage and each plant spreads to two feet. The blooms are white with a cherry polka-dot center and will cascade in hanging baskets or window boxes. Little Blanche is a snow white flower with no dark center. Others are also available in various shades of pink.

mixed. There are Cactus-flowered types, Dahlia-flowered, and a new bedding Zinnia called Peter Pan. They come in orange, scarlet, plum, pink, and a mixture and grow to twelve inches with three to four inch flowers.

Zinnias grow best in full sun and will need spraying against mildew during the seasonal temperatures that cause it. Other than that, they are among the most obliging and rewarding of annuals. They can be sown directly in early April where they are to flower, and for a fall follow-up, again in June. A good supply of Zinnias will be available at your garden center in ready-to-set-out plants.

Vinca Polka Dot.
Geo. W. Park Seed Co. photo.

40. Zinnia (3,000 seeds per ounce). Whatever role you wish this annual to perform, its color range is quite remarkable, from the tiny Thumbelina, which comes in two colors, Mini-Pink and Mini-Salmon, and grows six inches tall, to Giants growing to four feet tall with five to six inch flowers, such as the California Giants, obtainable in pink, rose, yellow, white, lavender, and

Azaleas

Both those plants commonly called Azaleas and those called Rhododendrons are properly members of the genus Rhododendron. Although there is no clear-cut differentiation, we commonly think of those with distinct clusters of flowers with ten or more stamens and large leaves as Rhododendrons, and those giving a mass appearance with five stamens in the flower and smaller, hairy leaves as Azaleas.

The deep south, from Charleston to Jacksonville and west to Mobile, monopolized the growing of Azaleas in America until the turn of the century. Together with Spanish Moss-laden live Oaks, they help typify pleasant living in this hemisphere.

The Indica species made famous the great plantations along the Ashley River in South Carolina, and such Gardens as Middleton and Magnolia Gardens became known the world over. Indica, or, as they are known, Indian Azaleas, came to America around 1838. Not until about 1920 was another great class of Azaleas introduced into the United States, the Japanese or Kurume Azaleas. Being much hardier, they soon were planted throughout the east and as far north as Boston.

Norfolk's famed Azalea Gardens, started in 1936 and now part of a botanical garden, has one of the world's best large collections of Azaleas, with over one hundred varieties in twelve

Norfolk's Azalea Gardens...
The Norfolk Botanical Gardens.

species. The plants number over 250 thousand, ranging from dwarfs less than a foot tall to twenty-five year old specimens over twelve feet high. These same Azaleas may be expected to grace the gardens for one hundred years or more.

Native Azaleas

There are also many native American Azaleas, most of them deciduous. Many of those native to the east coast of America are also natives of Zone 8.

The Roseshell Azalea, *R. roseum*, native from New England to Virginia, and the Pinxterbloom, from Maine to Florida, closely resemble one another. The Roseshell Azalea has a superior deep pink bloom which appears after the foliage has formed, whereas the pale pink Pinxterbloom blooms before the foliage appears as suggested by the name Nudiflorum.

The great Flame Azalea of the Blue Ridge mountains, *R. calendulaceum*, is not happy along the seashore, nor are the selections which have resulted from early crosses with its Tidewater cousin, Nudiflorum, generally known as Ghent Hybrids. The Flame Azalea is one of the most beautiful of our natives, growing from Pennsylvania to Georgia and reaching ten to twelve feet in height, particularly in the mountains. It has scentless flower clusters which vary from light yellow to bright red. In the fall its foliage turns various shades of yellow and bronze. It is more tolerant of dry soil than most Azaleas.

Another fine native of the mountains is the large Sweet Azalea, *R. arborescens*, a ten foot shrub with white fragrant blooms. It grows in moist soil from Pennsylvania to Alabama and Georgia.

Another parent of the Ghent Hybrids is the White Swamp Honeysuckle, *R. viscosum*. Its fragrant white or pink sticky flower clusters are the last wild Azaleas to appear in July, enriching the swamplands from Maine to South Carolina and Tennessee. It will also grow upland in drier locations and full sun.

The Cumberland Azalea, *R. cumberlandense,* appears several weeks after the Flame Azalea with deep orange red to orange flowers in the mountains of North Carolina and Virginia. The plants vary in size from six inch tall dwarfs to nine feet, but the usual height is from two to four feet.

The white clove-scented Hammocksweet Azalea, *R. serrulatum,* appears in June in moist woods from Southeast Virginia to Florida. Similar to the Pinxterbloom, the Florida Pinxter, *R. canescens,* blooms in April in moist coastal woodlands from Delaware to Florida and has honeysuckle-scented pink flowers. The Coast Azalea, *R. atlanticum,* is unusual in that it multiplies by horizontal underground stems forming colonies which produce clusters of white flowers on short-lived stems. This hardy Azalea appears along the coast from Pennsylvania to South Carolina.

Oriental Azaleas

The most tolerant, popular, and spectacular Azaleas, however, are the Oriental species which, when well located and established, play an important part in the beautification of Zone 8.

It is possible by judicious selection to have Azaleas in bloom from the last week in March to the end of June, although few varieties will hold in flower much over ten days.

Vittata fortunei, one of the early introductions (1870) of the Indicum hybrids, still remains the best early bloomer in late March. It is an upright grower ten or more feet tall with white

Azalea nudiflorum.

Vittata fortunei, Azalea.

or violet red flowers on the same bush, varied with flakes or stripes of both colors.

Closely following it in bloom, about the first week in April, is the tall growing *Kurume,* commonly called Flame, but not to be confused with the Flame Azaleas of the Calendulaceum group. This variety was among the famous fifty brought in by plant explorer Ernest H. Wilson and introduced in 1919. Its original name is Suetsumu, but Flame is so descriptive of its red color that it is generally listed as such.

Hinomayo, another of Wilson's fifty, is a delightful pink of medium growth which is most floriferous. This trio in perfect continuity constitutes the early blooming period, spanning no less than three weeks and preceding the main Azalea blooming season in mid-April when the Dogwood are in bloom.

Dogwood blooming time, ranging from mid-April to May in an average peak year, is most important to take into consideration when planning an Azalea display. One of the most vivid

performers of the original fifty Kurume Azaleas is Hinodegiri, a bright, crimson, low, compact grower. More plants have been sold of this variety than any other. A clone of this is now sold under the name Hino-Crimson together with Snow, its white counterpart.

About the same time the Hino Azaleas are in bloom, the variety *Indica alba,* sometimes known as *Ledifolia alba,* comes into bloom. It was introduced in England from China in 1819. Yet, as a good white to fit into this particular setting of Dogwoods and crimson Azaleas, it has no substitute.

As these fade from the picture, the most spectacular combination, in my estimation, comes into focus under the canopy of Dogwood, namely Pink Pearl and Formosa. Pink Pearl is a salmon rose Kurume variety of medium height described as hose-in-hose. Formosa, no doubt one of the most outstanding varieties, has red violet flowers over three inches in diameter on a tall spreading plant. In less than ten years, if given plenty of room, it will cover at least ten feet in height and width. The combination of Pink Pearl against

Formosa Pink Pearl.

Formosa under the white Dogwoods is a sight never to be forgotten. Omurasaki is almost identical to Formosa and may be substituted for it.

In an average season, when this combination disappears, the Dogwood petals are falling and a distinct break in the Azalea season seems to take place. It is adequately bridged by a variety not too well known but available as Salmon Queen, a *Mollis* hybrid. There are several reasons why Salmon Queen is valuable; it is evergreen in Zone 8 and is most attractive as a foliage plant which puts on a typical autumn display that is constant until new growth appears in the spring. In the full sun it will not fade or wilt as do most of the other late blooming varieties, and it appears in late April about the time Glacier, a dazzling white, opens. Glacier, in time, may replace *Indica alba* although it blooms later.

Until the Glenn Dale hybrid Azaleas were introduced in 1941, very few of the older varieties bridged the gap between Salmon Queen and the Macrantha season which begins in late May. An exception is a variety sold locally under the name of Rose Daphne, which is possible to find as "Lawsal," or under various synonyms such as Pride of Summerville and Daphne Salmon. A plant of medium growth, it generally blooms during the first week in May.

George Lindsey Taber, of medium height with white flowers flushed violet red with darker blotches, is one of the best growers to help fill that early May gap. It is a sport of Omurasaki.

Then a selection from hundreds of the Glenn Dale hybrids would include Everest, a lovely white with a pale chartreuse blotch; Margaret Hitchcock, an unusual white margined with ma-

Martha Hitchcock Azalea.

Carrard Azalea of the Glenn Dale hybrids. National Arboretum photo.

genta; Mary Margaret, rose with dots of purple in the upper lobe; Elizabeth, tyrian rose; and Nocturne, a dark purple with a blotch of rose.

Coccinea Major, an orange scarlet Indian Hybrid clone of the late 1870s, will fit into this seasonal lapse and fill in from mid-May to late May. These plants are vigorous growers, reaching five feet, with flowers to three inches in diameter.

During June the species *Macrantha*, also listed as Indicum, comes into bloom. It was cultivated in Japan for over three hundred years. The plain *Macrantha* variety has rose colored flowers two inches in diameter, closely

Macrantha Azalea.

placed on a low spreading plant. Specimens of this in the Norfolk Botanical Gardens are over thirty-five years old, but only three feet high and at least six feet across. A white form, Gumpo, grows only half that height and is most interesting with its frilled flowers nearly three inches in diameter.

There are many interesting varieties of these late blooming types, including Tanima-no-Yuki or Valley of Snow, having red to violet single flowers with white throats, and Sakuragata or Cherry Blossom.

Cultivation

Many factors affect the hardiness of Azaleas: the age of the plants, exposure, protection from houses and trees, snow coverage, quickness of temperature rise and fall, and mulches. Each particular situation must be judged for itself and oftentimes determined by trial and error.

More Azaleas die from deep planting than from climate variations or other ailments which befall their lot. Any amount of soil over a quarter of an inch above their topmost roots means slow suffocation. By nature,

Azaleas have very fine surface roots which are attracted by loose organic soil. Any deviation from this condition spells their doom. Therefore, proper placement as to depth and soil consistency is of utmost importance.

It is no exaggeration to state that the best medium for Azalea growth is a soil which is at least fifty per cent organic at the first foot level and sandy loam or sandy clay in the lower strata. It must be highly drained. The fifty per cent organic is best made up of hardwood leaves and Pine needles, or a combination of these with peat moss. No chemical fertilizer should be added to this mixture, although cottonseed meal, an organic fertilizer, will help to promote growth. This can be used at the rate of five pounds per hundred square feet of bed surface.

If the plants are set on soil which has been deeply excavated and is subject to settling, care must be taken to have the plants high enough to allow for this. In the case of transplanting large plants with heavy balls of earth, it is advisable that either the subsoil be thoroughly compacted or the plant placed on a few bricks or brickbats to prevent settling.

Azaleas are among the easiest shrubs to transplant. This can be done any time from October to April when temperatures are above freezing. In fact, many are handled successfully in full bloom when they are generally sold on the market.

Spacing is determined by the variety. The Indian Azaleas, which grow to ten feet if allowed, may be spaced five feet apart. Spacing also depends on how you wish to display your Azaleas. I have seen Formosa and other varieties of that species grown as specimens ten feet apart where space is available.

The average Kurume varieties for bed culture can be placed three to four feet apart and Indicas, five to six feet. They are easy to transplant, however, and you may wish to buy small plants and set them out half that distance for immediate effect and take every other plant out in a few years. These would make excellent gifts, if you have no room to expand, but under no circumstances should Azaleas be allowed to crowd one another out.

When the Azalea plant is in its final position it should be slightly above the surrounding ground level. This position will not be evident since mulch is placed over the ball and surrounding area.

Mulching Azaleas is a very important phase of their culture and can perhaps be best emphasized when it is understood that disintegrated mulch becomes soil. It is the essential diet in the life of an Azalea. While many kinds of mulch are acceptable,

Coral Bell Azalea at
Norfolk Botanical Gardens.

that made up of Pine needles, hardwood leaves, or their combination, proves the best. This material provides them with natural plant food. Ground up Pine bark is a new addition to the long list of waste material sold as mulch and seems to be a good substitute, although it has not been sufficiently tested by this writing.

Other mulch materials, which may range from peanut hulls to sawdust, may be acceptable as insulators, but do not possess in their decomposition what nature has provided in the plant's native habitat. When such mulches are used, it becomes necessary to subsidize their natural plant food with cottonseed meal or other organic fertilizers. This is also necessary when the plants must compete with surrounding trees or shrubs.

Fertilizing, however, particularly in late summer, may cause winter injury by stimulating soft new growth which does not have a chance to harden off before cold weather sets in. If any type of fertilizer is used, it should be applied immediately after blooming has finished.

If Zone 8's forty-inch rainfall were evenly distributed throughout the year, the watering of Azaleas would be no problem. Unfortunately, this seldom happens and thus during dry periods artificial watering must be done, another reason why adequate soil preparation with ample humus and mulching is imperative.

Azaleas, to thrive, should never be allowed to become dry, a condition soon indicated by wilting, and should be given frequent thorough soakings. The frequency of saturation will depend on the competition from nearby trees or stronger growing shrubs. Oaks and Maples will be tolerated by Azaleas if their moisture absorbing capacity in relation to the need of Azaleas is compensated for.

Under certain soil conditions, the foliage of Azaleas will turn light green. Iron chelates or micronized iron may be the answer, but the proper amount must be ascertained by having the soil tested. At the same time the soil may be tested for pH, or soil acidity, which should be about 5.5 or 6.0 for Azaleas.

In taking a soil sample, dig portions of soil from various parts of the bed, mix thoroughly together in a bucket, fill a quart jar with the mixture, and take to the laboratory for analysis.

Foliage discoloration may also be due to sucking insects such as lace bug, red spider, or white fly. Of course, this would be remedied by a proper spray program.

The death of a branch in late spring or summer may be caused by split bark just above ground level. The bark may split during periods of low temperature before the plant has hardened off. Injured flower buds may turn brown or fail to develop properly. In such a case, prune the branch back to healthy green growth.

Insects and Diseases

The three main insect enemies of Azaleas are red spider, white fly, and lace bug. Lace bug is particularly destructive, being the Azalea's number one enemy. Over-wintering broods will hatch about the time the plant is putting on its new growth. Consequently, the best time to spray is immediately after the flowers have fallen during April. May and later blooming varieties can be sprayed before flowering. Any good miticide

recommended under the law can be used effectively.

There are successive broods of both lace bug and red spider, and when heavy infestations are present another spray during June may be necessary. When the foliage of Azaleas becomes gray, it is no doubt an indication that either or both of these insects are present.

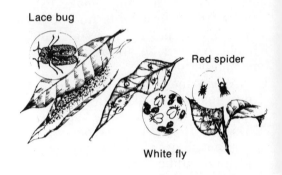

Lace bug

Red spider

White fly

Main Foes of broad-leaf evergreens.

Certain varieties of Azaleas, notably Indica Alba and Magnifica, are subject to infestation of white fly. The above spray schedule will kill them, but may need to be repeated in July and August. White flies seem to thrive on hot weather.

Unfortunately, the Azalea petal blight has also made its appearance. It is a disease entirely dictated by weather and atmospheric conditions. Diseases and insects must be treated separately. Both disease and insects can be readily controlled, but remain a matter of close timing, especially petal blight, which is noted by the flowers wilting as soon as they open, as though scalding water had been poured over them.

Flower or petal blight occurs only during periods of high humidity and abnormally high temperatures for the season. It seldom attacks the early bloomers for that reason and occurs in Zone 8 generally when Formosa and Pink Pearl are in bloom, from the middle to the end of April and thereafter.

Since the disease originates from tiny spores which are present at all times floating in the air, it can only be prevented during favorable periods by continually covering the flowers with a repellent. Petal blight fungicides are quite numeous. This disease does not affect the foliage or any other portion of the plant. Therefore, the fungicide should be directed to the flowers themselves, preferably as a fine mist. It is not the amount of spray that counts but its even distribution. The spray is most effective applied early in the morning when wind currents are at their lowest ebb and temperatures are low.

For complete coverage, the spray should be applied no less than twice a week or every third day while the plant is in bloom. Most sprays will not spot the flowers, as detected by the naked eye, if applied under fine mist.

Hexe, a beautiful red hose-in-hose Azalea variety, is subject to leaf gall. The galls appear when the new leaves develop as a swollen white cockscomb-like growth. This disease is best controlled by picking and burning the affected portions when first noted, then the next year spraying the plants as the new growth develops with a Bordeaux mixture.

Twig dieback, or a general decline of the plant, may be caused by nematodes. This is a complex problem which first must be diagnosed, then treated

Leaf gall on Hackberry Tree—normally not fatal but hard to control.

according to recommendations of local authorities.

Pruning

For some unknown reason many amateur gardeners do not seem to associate pruning with Azaleas, and, consequently, the plants soon outgrow their allocated space. Pruning, however, is an attribute of good Azalea culture and when necessary, after the plant has reached the desired size, should be done as soon as the plants have bloomed.

If you have overgrown plants, they will stand drastic pruning from two to six feet. Under such treatment it will take the plant one year to recuperate, and it may skip a year's bloom because the sucker growth will be so rapid that flower buds will not set. It is from this sucker growth, however, that the plant can be brought back to normal shape and size.

For an informal effect Azaleas should not be sheared, but pruned out to leave sufficient spacing between the terminal growth. After the plants are established and resume normal growth, Azaleas will develop as much as a foot per year in strong species like the Indicas, or as little as an inch in the variety Gumpo. Therefore, pruning should conform to the variety and not to a general pattern. Varieties such as Hino-degiri, which set seed heavily each year, should have the seedpods or tip growth removed as soon as they are through flowering.

Location

Most Azaleas prefer a semi-shaded location away from the midday sun, where they will last longer in bloom, especially those which open late. It is a fact, however, that they will bloom more profusely in the full sun. The plant will thrive in almost any location provided it is adequately mulched and supplied with moisture.

Azaleas are best located as understory plants to tall trees, preferably Pines. If you have no Pines, why not plant one to every two hundred square feet of Azalea bed? A small seedling Pine will do as it will soon outgrow the Azaleas and become their perfect companion and protector against sun, heat, and wind, besides eventually furnishing its best known diet of Pine needle mulch.

The Loblolly Pine is a good choice and should be transplanted as a one to two foot seedling in early spring along

George Lindsey Tabor Azalea.

with a Dogwood. Incorporate a Camellia here and there as an accent plant, add a few Daffodils, and you have the formula which has made the Norfolk Azalea Gardens famous. Periwinkle as a ground cover will complete the picture.

If you wish to expand your planting there are other native trees which will add beauty, such as the *Magnolia virginiana*, a handsome evergreen, or the *Gordonia lasianthus,* an evergreen with lovely fragrant white blooms from May throughout the summer. The spring blooming Fringetree, *Chionanthus virginica,* makes a welcome addition with its dainty white flowers along with Mountain Laurel, *Kalmia latifolia.* All grow in the same surroundings and soil condition.

A few other trees which will blend in well are the American Holly, *Ilex opaca,* for its red berries, the Deodar Cedar, *Cedrus deodara,* for its needled boughs of soft green, the native Myrtle, or any of the many Magnolias such as the Saucer Magnolia or Star Magnolia.

The hybrid Rhododendrons such as Cynthia or Michael Waterer are famous for their richly colored blooms in May, the *Pieris japonica* for its Lily-of-the-Valley type blossoms, or the *Mahonia aquifolium* for its Holly-like foliage and yellow blossoms. *Cephalotaxus,* or Plum Yew, is a rich dark green Yew-like plant which will blend well with Azaleas along with Pittosporum, Cherry Laurel, or the fragrant *Viburnum odoratissimum.* For a tropical touch, the fall blooming *Fatsia japonica,* or Aralia, adds a lush beauty.

To add further interest throughout the seasons many perennials such as Columbine, Coral Bells, or Galax may be added for their lovely flowers, or *Arum italicum* and *Arum maculatum* for their interesting arrow-shaped foliage in the winter. Of course, such bulbs as the Turkscap Lily, Scilla, dainty Lycoris, Amarillis, or the autumn-blooming Crocus, Colchicum, and Sternbergia, would always be a welcome addition.

Azaleas are long-lived, some spanning a century or more, provided they have been located and planted properly and given such annual care as spraying, pruning, fertilizing, and watering. Most casualties occur from deep planting and over-fertilizing with chemical additives. If the danger points are observed and a good selection is made, much satisfaction and pleasure will be derived from their incorporation in the home garden.

Camellias

Part One:

Introduction To Camellias

While Camellias were first grown out of doors in the vicinity of Charleston, South Carolina, around 1790, they have by now well saturated the extent of our representative map and even beyond, with some of the hardier types grown successfully in protected areas of Long Island, New York, and New Jersey. Their migration from the Orient, westward through the British Isles to our shores, was rather slow at first, but by the turn of this century they had crossed the Mason-Dixon Line, and today two of the best collections on the east coast are located in Norfolk, Virginia and at the National Arboretum in Washington, D.C.

There are many reasons why every garden located within Zone 8 should include Camellias; they are truly representative of their native habitat, and no other plant can take their place at the time of year when they best perform. I hope that by the time you read about this magnificent genus, whose evolution has been a special study of mine for the past forty years, you will be convinced that they merit special attention. What a joy to have flowers from September to May when few evergreens have the stamina to open their blossoms, especially during the shortest days of the year.

By cultivating Camellias in the modern garden, we become a part of their mystic past, covering centuries in the Orient. Plant explorers and historians have fascinating tales to tell about searching out the unknown and exotic varieties of this species. Only recently have we acquired many of our most precious specimens since apparently both China and Japan, for the past two hundred years, have given us only those which they thought most inferior.

During that time, however, both European and American gardeners, using the few Camellias known to them, have produced some remarkable hybrids, which together with later introductions surpass anything produced in the Orient. Today we have offered in commerce over two thousand varieties in dozens of species and subspecies. It is from this maze that I will attempt to acquaint you with those which I believe are best to get you started on a fall and winter wonderland.

From the colder regions we have learned that the hardiest of the true species is the *Camellia japonica* with the *Camellia sasanqua* a close second. It is from these two species that I have chosen nine favorite varieties which span the blooming period from September to May, and represent the wide color range available. These plants are the easiest and hardiest for beginning Camellia growers, but a more complete selection is described in Part Three.

September normally opens with

the *Camellia japonica* variety, Are-jishi, which translates restive lion and was introduced in Japan in 1891. Its flower is a dark salmon rose, medium sized to three inches. It is a vigorous plant, open and upright, which grows to ten feet. There is also a variegated clone available which is streaked rose and white. While well-established older plants will sometimes have a few blooms in August, and even a few at the end of march, October is the best blooming month.

Diakagura, which means great sacred dance, is another Japonica introduced by the Japanese in 1891. This plant of slow compact growth has a rose pink, splotched white blossom with a medium to large Peony form up to four inches. When established, its best blooming period is October, November, and December.

During October and November the fall blooming species Sasanqua also makes its appearance, and if I were limited to one variety, I would without hesitation recommend Papaver, not particularly well known but ideal for this climate. It will produce soft pink single blossoms over an inch in dia-

Shishi-Gashira.
American Camellia Society photo.

meter. These are cupped in form and produced along the top of the stems, consecutively from October through the New Year. The plant itself has a sprawling form, which makes it advisable to place it in front of the larger growing types.

To complete the color and plant size range for September to January we must include a variety of the species *Hiemalis* called Shishi-Gashira, translated from the Japanese as lion's head. It has a small flower of semi-double form in a deep red. Its main characteristic as a plant is that it will not grow over three feet tall and has a sprawling habit which makes it suitable for a hanging basket.

To adequately bridge the New Year, a time when temperatures drop below freezing, we turn to the species *Vernalis* and a variety called Dawn, Gin-Ryu in Japanese. It produces semi-double white flowers suffused with pink of two to two and one-half inches in diameter. This plant has a tall growing habit to ten feet with beautiful glossy small foliage of which portions will often variegate. Dawn makes beautiful flowering hedges by planting the shrubs five feet apart and keeping them to half their size through judicious annual pruning when they have finished flowering in early March. An amazing variety, it starts blooming in early December and is covered by an avalanche of white blossoms. Its main characteristic, however, is the capacity of its open flowers to withstand as much as five degrees below freezing; if below that, Dawn recoups quickly when temperatures go back to normal and is an excellent bloomer and performer for January and February. However this variety will winter-kill

Dawn.
American Camellia Society photo.

up the eastern shore of Virginia. A counterpart to its performance is Hiryo, Redbird, of the same species. To see the small double crimson flowers performing under a blanket of snow is indeed a rewarding sight.

The Camellia japonica variety Lady Clare, which is being sold erroneously as Empress, is perhaps the greatest all-around performer for Zone 8. It begins to bloom in January and will still win blue ribbons in April. The four to five inch flowers are deep pink semi-double in form, with prominent yellow stamens often interspersed with what are called rabbit ears in Camellia parlance, making it an intriguing flower.

Lady Clare, which flowers profusely, is a most vigorous and broad plant with unusual glossy and large foliage. An old Japanese variety, first introduced in England in 1887 from whence it came to America, it has produced many sports, such as Nelly Bly, Onigi, Destiny, and Linda Loughlin. While the flowers of Lady Clare will not stand the low temperatures of

Dawn, if under a canopy of tall Pines, it will stand freezing weather with the unopened flower buds recouping quickly when temperatures rise. These are the characteristics that place Lady Clare and Dawn above others as winter bloomers for our zone, at least from my standpoint, after thirty-five years of studying the entire genus.

To complete these eight months of floral splendor in the garden I would include Mathotiana, which normally blooms best in March and April. This variety of the Japonica species originated as a chance seedling in the Magnolia Gardens near Charleston, South Carolina, in 1840. Perhaps no other Camellia has ever approached its record of producing progeny, some of which are even superior in size and color to the parent plant. Mathotiana is often sold as Julia Drayton, Purple Dawn, or Emperor, for just like famous people, popular Camellias have many imitators. As a plant, it is very vigorous

Mathotiana.
American Camellia Society photo.

and tall; some one hundred year old specimens have grown over fifteen feet tall and nearly as broad. As with Lady Clare, Mathotiana prefers a canopy of tall Pines to display its natural splendor. Its flowers, crimson with a purple cast, are spectacular as they grow to six inches in diameter with a perfect rose form, showing stamens only when several days old.

An equally famous Camellia variety which rivals Mathotiana as a progenitor is Elegans, originated in 1831 by Lord Chandler of England, hence often sold under the name of Chandler's Elegans. It has a spreading growth habit and produces six inch Anemone-shaped flowers in spotted rose pink or marbled white. This is also normally a late bloomer. The progeny of this variety are so numerous that they require a family tree all their own. One of these, C. M. Wilson, is a light pink sport introduced in the United States in 1949. Other progeny from these crosses are C. M. Wilson Splendor and Shiro-Chan, both bearing Anemone-shaped blossoms with the former a light pink variegated color and the latter nearly pure white. It is easy to see from this one variety how each species can saturate the color and size range of the Camellia genus.

As with all plants, whether Camellias or Roses, I am always asked to select one which would be the hardiest and most fool-proof. So I shall end this selection with Tricolor Sieboldii. This Camellia, known originally as Wakanoora variegated, was bred in Japan and introduced to the western world through Germany in 1832, where the commercialized name Siebold was added. One of the latest to bloom, its attractiveness is due to its semi-double

Tricolor Siebold.
American Camellia Society photo.

flowers, white streaked with carmine in many combinations which often vary on the same plant, hence Tricolor. It is a slow growing variety on the compact side, has been known to stand below-zero temperatures, and will also tolerate full sun exposure, which most Camellias will not. It, too, has many progeny, including a lovely pure white sport called Leucantha, or Tricolor White. It originated in the United States in 1937 over a hundred years after Tricolor was brought from Japan.

This selection is entirely geared to intrigue the beginners and keep their interest from September to May. We now offer a more sophisticated list, including some with idiosyncrasies.

Part Two:
Some Idiosyncrasies of the
Genus Camellia

Camellias are a large genus including no less than twenty-five species with thousands of varieties in commerce here and abroad. It must be noted that to avoid confusion most names and descriptions are those taken from the Thirteenth Revised Edition of the book *Camellia Nomenclature,* adapted as the official document of the American Camellia Society.

The last Camellia species to be discovered was Granthamiana, found in Hong Kong new territory in 1955 and named in honor of Sir Alexander Grantham, the former governor of the colony. It bears handsome flowers which measure five and one-half inches in diameter and bloom through November and December. The flowers are most unusual with eight to ten pure white petals forming almost an aura around a conspicuous golden yellow stamen cluster. Its foliage is unlike most other Camellia species and was at first confused with that of the Gordonia genus. Its leaves are oblong-elliptic with a pointed apex, in a texture reminiscent of some of the evergreen Viburnums. The plant grows quite fast and has withstood temperatures down to fifteen degrees, which in a sense belies its origin in the Hong Kong province where, incidentally, only one plant was ever found.

Norfolk, Virginia has good reason to claim Camellia Granthamiana; without a doubt, this city introduced it to the western world and actually produced its first American bloom. In 1956, as director of the Norfolk Botanical Gardens, I negotiated with the Hong Kong Botanical Garden to obtain a tip-scion, which Robert Matthews, now superintendent of the gardens, grafted on a Sasanqua understock. It became the progenitor of all those now in the Tidewater gardens and throughout the eastern United States.

I am particularly indebted to the Granthamiana and consider its introduction into this country the turning point of my career. When the first flower appeared on the Norfolk Gardens' plant in 1959, I had a local florist arrange it to best display its magnificent blossom and took it to a meeting of the Board of Directors of the National

Granthamiana.

Arboretum in Washington, D.C. The scientists stood in awe, and this discovery led to many exciting events in my career.

The status of Granthamianas indicates how plants often take quite a while to gain momentum and become available to home gardeners; as they are still not sold in commerce on the eastern seaboard. Nevertheless, this species remains one of the most spectacular Camellias during its blooming period, which reaches its peak in December. It survived the winter of 1972-73, one of the most disastrous in modern times, while other plants, supposedly hardier. The winter of 1977 in Zone 8 seems to have taken its toll of this magnificent species, but as of July 1977 the original plant is recuperating.

One of the loveliest of the older southern Camellias, Debutante, with light pink, Peony-shaped blossoms, was originated in the Magnolia Gardens near Charleston in 1900. It had been practically discarded in Virginia and Washington until the introduction of gibbing. This practice is particularly useful to gardeners in the northern limits of our zone where older, generally southern varieties whose blossoms are not winter hardy can be made to bloom sixty to eighty days ahead of schedule, which would normally be during the most inclement weather of January and February. Mathotianas and Blood of China, among the latest varieties to bloom in the spring, can also be made to bloom in November and December, ninety to one hundred days before their normal blooming cycle.

Perhaps the most intriguing idiosyncrasy of Camellia growth is mutation, or the fundamental change in heredity. This, no doubt, has been responsible for more new varieties than any cross breeding or scientific manipulation, and has only been recognized by horticulturists for the past 144 years.

For example, Elegans, mentioned under basic selections, has no less than thirty descendants on its family tree, most of which are mutants. The peculiar part is that it does not take any expertise on anyone's part to produce another mutant, and there is always a chance that it may happen to you. When a parent plant has set seeds that are cross-pollinated by other Camellias in the area, their progeny will rarely reproduce the characteristics of the parent plants, and it is estimated that one in a thousand will be as good as the parent, and one in ten thousand will be superior. However, superior plants are known and a miracle you can always hope for.

It is advisable to salvage such seeds or seedlings to be used within five years as understock for grafting. Dig the seedlings up when a year old, or sow the seeds in eight to ten inch pots.

Elegans.
American Camellia Society photo.

The history of Camellias is fascinating, if not fantastic. For instance, the history of the modern Rose only goes back to Empress Josephine in the late eighteenth century, whereas there are authentic records that Camellias were being hybridized in Japan in 1200 A.D. This may have been preceded in China, for as recently as World War II, a Britisher accidentally discovered a rare selection of the Camellia species, Reticulata, which had been cultivated for hundreds of years within the cloistered walls of monasteries in the Yuman Province. There were ten original varieties of the species imported in 1958 by the late Ralph S. Peer of Hollywood, California, a Camellia enthusiast who has done perhaps more than any other amateur to bring this genus to the forefront in America.

For the record, the names are Crimson Robe, Tali-Queen [turkey red to deep pink], Cornelian [a variegated form of Lion Head], Moutancha [bright pink veined with white], Purple Gown [dark purple-red with pink stripes], Butterfly Wings [rose pink], Willow Wand [orchid pink], Shot Silk, Spinel Pink, and Professor Tsai [rose pink].

Eventually, after due propagation, the original ten sold at one thousand dollars per collection. The Norfolk Botanical Gardens became recipient of one of these through the generosity of the late Mrs. C. W. Grandy. To my knowledge only one person in Tidewater, Mrs. M. K. Crockett of Virginia Beach, has successfully cultivated them out of doors, although quite a few are grown indoors.

All ten varieties have flowers that range up to ten inches in diameter and are mostly semi-double to Peony-shaped with large to very large wavy petals of which some are crinkled and crape-like. No other flower approaches its sophistication. Often people, when seeing them on exhibit, will ask, "Are these real flowers?"

While the plants are vigorous, they are not as well organized in structure as are most other Camellias, which may be why they have not become more popular in outdoor landscaping in our zone. They grow better out of doors on the west coast where they have received considerable attention from plant breeders who have added possibly a hundred or more varieties to the original collection. One of these, Budah, known for its vigorous upright growth, has a very large, semi-double blossom with wavy pink petals. This interspecific hybrid, having been crossed with the species *C. pitardii*, has received a plant patent.

Before leaving the Reticulatas, mention should be made that prior to importing the Peer Collection, a variety of the same species, Captain Rawes, had been introduced in England in 1820, was well known to eastern United States Camellia collectors, and was prospering in Tidewater, Virginia.

One of the lesser known facts concening Camellias is that the genus is closely related to the commercial Tea plant. *Camellia thea,* with white scented flowers, will survive as far north as Tidewater, Virginia, but will never attain the size tree it does in its native habitat of Asia.

Two of the greatest goals of horticultural researchers are the development of a scented Camellia and one with a true yellow flower. When both of these goals have been accomplished, Camellias will have reached their zenith.

Part Three:
Camellias Worth Noting

It is quite brash for one individual to dictate a list of Camellias which would purport to be all-inclusive even for a specialized area, Zone 8. It is even harder to distinguish those which are best for landscape effect from those primarily used for cut flowers or show purposes. Nevertheless, as books are normally written in that vein, and because of my life long fascination as well as my forty years experience in dealing with them, I will attempt to offer a basic seasonal selection.

An early bloomer, Betty Sheffield, was introduced in 1949 and has produced many mutations, my favorite being Betty Sheffield Supreme of 1962. This variety and its many sports should be scrutinized even if you can only include one from this famous clan. The original has slightly waved petals, of medium to large semi-double to loose Peony form in white with variegations of blotched red and pink.

The mutation, Supreme, is blush-pink with a wide edge of deep pink to red. There are no less than a dozen Betty Sheffields offered on the market, each with a different appeal. It responds well to gibbing and can be made to bloom during December while its natural season is March.

Donckelarii is a very old variety, first produced in Belgium by the famous horticulturist Siedbold in 1834, and still winning prizes as the best in the show. It has white semi-double flowers which are marbled red in various degrees. There are many named strains of this variety, all of which have a slow, bushy growth pattern. One of its most famous sports is

Ville de Nantes, which was introduced in France in 1910, and has also produced many named strains. Its upright, fimbriated petals are medium to large semi-double in form and have a dark red color, blotched with white.

Dr. Tinsley is an eye catcher in a very pale pink shade with deeper pink edges and a reverse side of flesh pink. It has medium sized, semi-double flowers with compact, upright growth, and normally blooms in March.

Drama Girl, a Japonica which originated on the west coast in 1950, has a very large, six or more inches, semi-double flower of deep salmon and grows vigorously in a pendulous conformation.

Elegans Supreme, a sport of the Elegans mentioned in our basic collection, originated in the United States in 1960. It has rose pink petals with very deep serrations.

Guilio Nuccio, also a west coast introduction in Sacramento, California, in 1875, has vigorous upright growth. Its pink petals with irregular white borders streaked in deep pink are semi-double in a medium-sized formation. A March bloomer, it improves with gibbing and can be had in bloom in December. It has many progeny and is one of the few Camellias which has a slight fragrance.

Hishi-Karaito, translated from the Japanese to mean thread of diamonds or stamens, is unusual because its small flower grows only from two to two and one-half inches. The delicate pink, semi-double petals with mixed petaloids make it an excellent boutonniere. Hishi-Karaito can be kept to three or four feet of compact growth, making it most suitable for containers.

Mathotiana is described under the

basic collection, and I would also like to recommend one of its many clones, Mathotiania Supreme, which was introduced in the United States in 1951 and normally takes top prize for the size of its flowers. I have picked gibbed blooms in my yard over six inches in diameter with loose semi-double irregular petals interspersed with stamens of the same color as its parent plant, which is crimson with a purple cast.

Pink Perfection, imported from Japan in 1875 and perhaps one of the better known of the old varieties according to national survey, is still winning top prizes. It has a formal double flower of an unusual bright pink, and while the flowers are small compared to others they are most floriferous on an upright growing plant which can either be used as a hedge or in the landscape as a specimen.

Rosea Superba is a sport of Mathotiana originating in Europe in 1890, while the parent was found in Charleston, South Carolina, in 1840. Its formation is identical to its progenitor except it has a pure rose pink flower. Another close to this is Rosea Superba Variegated, which has white spots.

Sawada's Dream is perhaps the most sophisticated, if we can apply such a label to a Camellia, and was bred by one of America's greatest Camellia authorities and plantsmen in 1958. It must be seen to be appreciated, as the medium size, formal, double white petals have one third of their outer petals shaded a delicate pink.

Tomorrow is another flower which is spectacular when placed on an exhibition table especially when gibbed. The very large semi-double, irregular petals and large petaloids are Strawberry red. The plant, introduced in the United States in 1953, is vigorous, open, and slightly pendulous, and has many sports.

I would be remiss in my discussion of Camellias if I did not mention a few that I believe are best suited as landscape plants, with a few others thrown in for their unusual adaptation for specific uses.

Perhaps we should start with one which was a chance seedling discovered by Mrs. Lyman Clarke, for whom it was named in 1949. The flowers are white-shaded orchid pink of medium semi-double to Peony form. It has two outstanding characteristics; it is a late bloomer, practically ending the Camellia season, and has a tall pyramid form which stands full exposure to the sun. I mention this because plants of the same species do not always behave alike, and apparently the rest of the Camellia world has never popularized this Norfolk belle which I believe is the best landscape variety available.

From the Sasanquas we can name many which hold their own with any plant in the landscape. They are durable and can stand full exposure, making them ideal for informal hedges. Very flexible stems make some of them suitable for espaliering, and they are so heat resistant they can even stand a southern exposure with reflected heat from a dwelling. Consider, for instance, Mine-No-Yuki, or Snow on the Mountain as translated from the Japanese, which blooms in abundance from November to December with flowers in double Peony form about an inch in diameter. There are also two other pink forms of this, Pink Snow and Pink Princess, which have the same habits and adaptability.

You might wish a specimen plant

of Cleopatra on your front lawn with its multitudes of rose pink semi-double flowers, or Hinode-Gumo with large white single flowers shaded pink. Both of these plants are very vigorous and upright growers with glossy evergreen foliage which should be allowed to grow to the ground. They eventually reach ten to twelve feet in height and nearly as much in width.

Few home gardeners realize that some Sasanquas can be used for hanging baskets and ground covers such as Showa-No-Sakae, Tanya, a rose pink single, White Frills, and Bonanza, a deep red. These could be used as foreground planting or low hedges.

Unquestionably, if you are looking for a group of plants that will put color in your landscape from September to May with a few interruptions during the inclement periods of winter, you should search among the Camellia genus.

Part Four:
Camellia Culture

While the description of the culture of Camellias can be oversimplified, it can still be summed up in one paragraph.

Locate them under high filtered sunlight in rich organic soil on well drained land and never let them lack for moisture. Because Camellias are slow starters, it will be around ten years before you can expect their magnificent performance. On the other hand, from then on they will require annual attention, especially pruning.

Most Camellia species grow in their native habitats under filtered sunlight. Our own native Pines best

simulate this environment and are good companion trees to Camellias because they strip themselves of their lower limbs and provide high light, have a long tap root which never stops until it strikes water, and, unlike Oaks and other hardwoods, have few surface roots to compete with other plants.

Therefore, if you do not have this environment for your Camellias, you would do well to provide it by inter-planting some native Pines to grow up with your Camellias. The Pines can be secured from almost any nursery, from heights of a couple of feet to as tall as you wish, depending on what you plan to spend. They can be planted ten feet apart and after that magic ten years I mentioned, every other one can be cut down.

Besides the filtered sunlight the Pines will provide, the annual crop of needles falling to the ground will supply the Camellias with their needed source of mulch which provides food value in the ever increasing amounts that they demand. In addition, the needles keep the pH level to around 5-5, a condition best suited for both the Pines and Camellias, and an added bonus is weed control. It is that simple to meet a Camellia's needs after it has been planted.

The initial planting of Camellias is most important and, done correctly, will insure future success. Even if you are blessed with an established Pine grove you will need to improve the soil since Pines will thrive on a much leaner diet than Camellias.

Camellias must have a rich organic soil for the deployment of their root system which is primarily made up of fibrous root-hairs. The formula I suggest is equal parts heavy loam, peat moss or compost, and sand or vermiculite. This can be modified to meet your existing conditions.

The quantity of this booster soil mix will of course vary with the size of plants you are handling, but should be no less than a bushel per plant even if that plant comes out of a quart container. Speaking of containers, be sure to remove these before setting out your plant. I highly recommend the ball and burlapped plants grown in nurseries rather than those sold in cans.

Setting out the plant is most important and the Camellia must be planted in such a manner that it will never settle below the existing level of the contours of the garden. This condition can be affected by adding enough booster soil to the hole to elevate the roots of the new plant. Make sure that you prepare your hole several weeks in advance of planting so that the soil will have a chance to settle. For the same reason, it should also be well watered down before setting out your plant; otherwise, your Camellia will suffer slow suffocation.

Adequate drainage is important and can be quite simply determined by the home gardener. Using a posthole digger, dig a hole at least three feet deep and fill it with water. If it does not drain out in fifteen minutes, you may have a serious problem. Your county agricultural agent or local expert can suggest pipes, culverts, and involved designs that will eliminate drainage problems permanently but which will involve considerable effort and expense. I have found a most effective way to provide drainage for individual plants and small areas that is easy enough for the home owner to implement.

After preparing a hole for the Camellia, or any other shrub for that matter, take a post hole digger and puncture the clay strata which is responsible for the poor drainage. This may be two to five feet below ground surface, but you will know when you have reached it. Fill the punctured hole with bricks or gravel, and the larger hole with enough booster soil to insure the elevation of the crown of the plant. In a small area where already established plants are suffering from poor drainage, several deep clay punctures located away from root systems will solve your problems. Bricks work particularly well in drainage holes since they are very porous and will provide some stored up moisture to your plants during dry periods.

All of these precautions will insure the long life span for which Camellias are so well known. For example, the first Camellia which was permanently

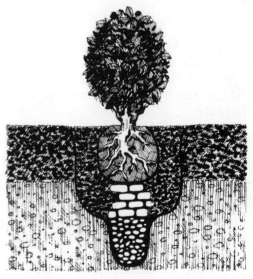

Planting to prevent plant from settling and provide additional drainage.

planted in the United States, in the vicinity of Charleston, South Carolina, has survived since the late eighteenth century, and many plantings in the Orient date back several hundred years. To satisfy even our own generation we must not only plant them well but give them sufficient room to develop.

As noted, Camellias are slow starters as seen in an average commercial plant which is probably only twenty-four to thirty inches high although three to four years old. The small size, which normally flowers, is recommended over a larger plant, not only for economic reasons but for its recuperative ability.

When a Camellia is purchased from a nursery, which generally guarantees it for a year, and is planted as recommended, adequate moisture alone will keep it growing for the first several years. During this time it needs no additional plant food or pruning other than removing the spent blooms which might set seed production and retard its annual growth.

By the time Camellias are about ten years old they will start to require annual pruning because they are reaching their full potential, with the average variety growing as much and even more than one foot a year. This will continue until they reach their maximum size, which may be from ten to fifteen feet tall and as broad in some varieties.

This ten year or five-foot period is the critical time when you must decide how tall and broad you wish them to grow. Through judicious pruning they can be kept indefinitely within the range you desire. By no means does this mean that they should be trimmed with hedge shears which entirely defeats their purpose of producing beautiful flowers on graceful stems.

In case you have not pruned your Camellias let me quickly emphasize that it is never too late, because when good shrubs that are well planted fall prey to neglect they will withstand drastic cutting back and live on to produce again and reign in splendor. Even drastic pruning to within a couple of feet above ground with a pruning saw will not defeat their recuperative powers.

The main technique in keeping established plants healthy and productive throughout their life span is to keep their superstructure open through pruning enough to permit air circulation. Maturing plants will produce an overabundance of twiggy growth which should be removed or it will

leader

Preserve leader (if wanted) by removing competitive side branches.

become a harbor for pests and diseases. The annual pruning I recommend is done immediately after a variety has completed its blooming period, spreading the work-load throughout several months.

When this has been accomplished, you then predetermine whether you wish the plant to grow taller or be restricted to a certain size. In the latter case the leaders are pruned back to one-quarter of an inch from a growth bud pointing in the direction you wish the plant to grow. Camellia's root systems are so strong that their recuperative growth is generally phenomenal, which is the reason I call this method "feeding through the pruning shears."

Accumulated dead twigs and branches of neglected Camellias not only harbour scale and other insects, but result in diseases such as dieback, which is nature's way of keeping the plant in balance, but certainly not the right way. During the annual clean up, you naturally will notice whether the plant has accumulated scale or other defects, and thus control it at its source.

If any plant's root system has ventured into unfavorable ground, this too can be detected by the yellowing of the leaves, and should be remedied by catering to its diet. A sprinkling of cotton-seed meal, an organic fertilizer, will do wonders to keep them healthy. Use it at a rate of one pound to each two feet of the plants' height up to five feet. Plants over five feet should receive a pound per foot, and a ten foot plant can readily assimilate ten pounds a year if it needs it. Remember, by that time, the canopy of Pine trees you have

provided will also be giving them a bonus. It is also interesting to note that healthy Camellias, in the proper environment, rarely need fertilizer since they manufacture their own food through the peculiar formation of their root system. This process is called mychoriza and is the reason that chemical fertilizers can sometimes harm the shrubs.

As noted under general recommendations in this book, an amateur should never try to out-guess nature, therefore if we have not covered the proper spray or feeding techniques within the monthly work schedule, take your questions to a professional.

Because the feeder roots of Camellias are near the surface, they become resentful of any disturbances, hence mulching is the best medium to accommodate them. As previously mentioned, Pine needles are a recommended additive, although other mulches such as ground-up Pine bark and even sawdust will suit them. The greatest contribution mulch of any kind makes is to retain moisture. Camellias, especially until well established, demand adequate moisture. This points out the necessity for a good watering program throughout the season in which they bloom, for once in a while we have drought periods during the winter.

One of the worst diseases to attach itself to Camellias is flower blight, which incidentally occurs at the peak of their main flowering season during March. It is entirely caused by the atmospheric conditions which normally occur then. Temperatures suddenly rising above sixty-five or seventy degrees during times of high humidity cause the fungus

Sclerotinia to spread. It does not harm the plant itself, but mars the opened blossom. The best antidote is the application of a fungicide (consult your local authority for an appropriate type) over the flowers from the time they are partially open for as long as the conditions persist. This may require misting two to three times a week during such intervals. Incidentally, this does not disfigure the flower itself.

Pests and disease are really small problems if Camellias are provided with the proper environment and annual pruning. The plants are hardy throughout our zone and will even perform in glory after severe neglect. They are a most satisfactory shrub for any purpose.

Another of the benefits of Camellias is their ability to provide their owners with ever increasing variety at small or no cost at all. This is achieved through the process of grafting, a method known since time immemorial and easily performed by the average gardener. A new variety of Camellia may cost up to fifty dollars commercially, but through grafting the desired progeny can be blooming within two years for practically nothing.

The materials needed for performing this technique are a bamboo stake, garden wire, a screwdriver, a sharp knife, an understock, which is usually a five-year old seedling either sown or grown wild under the parent Camellia, and a scion, which is the tip end of the new variety you are propagating.

I recommend using the cleft grafting method, which basically describes the way in which you cut the stem of the scion into a sharp wedge shape.

Before grafting onto the understock be sure that the shrub is well pruned and open to sunlight and air. Choose several branches that constitute the main body of the plant, remembering that the ideal size is from one-half inch to one inch in diameter which allows the scion to catch up within two years. I do not advocate using a larger stock as often practiced. Even pencil-sized understock can be used as a grafting medium although the scion will need to be tied in place since there is not sufficient pressure to hold it as in the case of the larger ones.

Once you have chosen the proper understock, split it about one inch deep and pry it open with a screwdriver to receive the scion. Then carefully place the stem tip into the split. The trick is to be certain that the cambium layers, the greenish band close to the bark outside of the stems, are in line with each other. The pressure of the understock will keep the scion in place until ready in about six weeks. For insurance use two scions, one on each side of the understock, because if water lodges in the open crevices, rot often sets in. Once the graft has taken and the new growth is vigorous remove the extra scion or the two will crowd each other.

During the healing process of the understock and scion a cellophane or plastic bag and sphagnum moss are secured to them with bamboo canes and garden wire to maintain moisture and prevent wind damage. The stakes are tied in a tripod fashion to hold the thoroughly soaked moss around the graft, and this is covered with a plastic bag which is large enough to allow six inches of air space around the scion.

As an added protection, a paper bag is placed over the cellophane bag and left there for a month, which is the period required for the initial healing process. It is then carefully removed, and by that time the scion will be evident. The cellophane bag is not removed until sufficient new growth touches the top of the bag. Six weeks to two months from grafting time will have to elapse before the union is completed. After removing the bag, it is wise to leave the splints and sphagnum for another month to prevent possible physical disturbance. By that time the cambium layer will have entirely enveloped the union.

The ideal time for grafting is early March, after all fear of frost has passed. However, it can be performed until late spring. Whatever time is chosen the important factor in grafting is the union of the cambium layers. If this is accomplished, nature will do the rest.

An appealing aspect of the Cammellia genus is their capacity to be grown as a tubbed plant within the limits of your lifting powers, say up to an eighteen inch size. When they outgrow their container they can be set out of doors in a permanent emplacement. In fact this is an excellent starting point for any of the varieties mentioned.

Many garden centers offer Camellias in containers; you simply grow them out of doors during the frost-free months, then retire them to a frost-free porch or greenhouse for enjoyment at all other times. They will flower for you as long as they are in a daytime temperature between freezing and sixty degrees.

Camellias possess a strong fibrous root system which will soon fill up and absorb the nourishment contained in an eighteen inch redwood tub, but through

a judicious feeding and pruning schedule can be so contained for at least ten years.

Purchase Camellias during their flowering season in one to three gallon containers and place them in a fifteen to eighteen inch redwood tub with a two inch layer of drainage material such as rough Pine bark lining the bottom.

The initial mixture of soil varies from that recommended for outdoor culture because the addition of equal parts of topsoil is necessary for the bulk in the container. It would pay to purchase this mixture already sterilized; all garden centers carry it as potting soil. Add one-third peatmoss and one-third ground-up Pine bark to each bushel of this mixture and thoroughly mix in one pint of Osmocote, a fertilizer which is very slow in releasing its balanced ingredients. Any young Camellia placed in this mixture would need no added food for the first season after planting. Because this mixture is very light, an eighteen-inch tub can readily be handled.

The trick of growing Camellias in tubs rests entirely in adequate care, headed by ample moisture. They will need copious amounts, especially when they have filled the container with roots, normally occurring within one year after planting.

Up to this period little is needed as to pruning other than removing spent blooms. No further application of fertilizer is necessary until after the first flush of growth has been completed in July. From then on Camellias are in the process of developing their flower buds, and any earlier fertilization would tend to cultivate premature leaf and stem formations. Some growers advocate a sixteen percent super-phosphate formula to more or less arrest their growth during the pre-bud plant formation, and this may have some merit.

However, catering to their bud-forming stage seems sufficient for container grown plants. To achieve this, I would advocate a fertilizer such as 10-10-10 in small dosages as a monthly feeding program until that particular variety comes into bloom; then stop for that season. There are many formulas on the market, and your selection will in most part depend on your own observation of the success of any particular application. Liquid fertilizers are perhaps the best and easiest to apply.

Keeping tubbed Camellias in good form is, of course, an art unto itself, and the ten-year span mentioned is an average lifetime. During that period an annual pruning similar to the proce-dure discussed for outdoor pruning would be in order following their flowering sequence.

When summering the Camellias out of doors, the most logical place for each tub is a cinder block or brick foundation. A semi-shaded location is best, as afforded by a canopy of Pine trees or a lath-house. When watering, do not be timid, for they will relish overhead sprinkling from a spray under normal water pressure at fre-quent intervals.

Before moving your Camellias to their winter quarters, it would be advisable to subject them to some cold weather, including some light freezing. They are essentially outdoor plants, most of them originating from climates akin to ours.

You are sure to enjoy Camellias indoors, especially the Reticulatas, which are the jewels of their genus or perhaps the entire kingdom of plants. At least the Camellia world will attest to this, and welcome any challenge from a Rose enthusiast.

The Magic of Gibberellic Acid

In 1828, T. A. Konishi of Japan, a plant physiologist, discovered that a malady of the rice plant caused defective rice seedlings to grow taller than healthy plants, but prevented them from producing grain at matur-ity. The responsible plant hormone was isolated and by 1959 experi-ments justified its use to promote growth on other plants. Among these was the Camellia, and in ten years, with the commercialization of gibbe-rellic acid, a new departure in the growing of Camellias was launched.

The effect of this chemical could be called magic, because when applied it not only accelerates the plant's blooming schedule by as much as

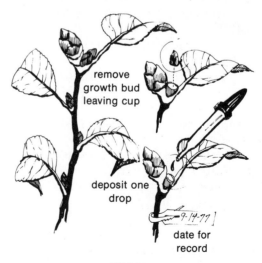

remove growth bud leaving cup

deposit one drop

date for record

Gibbing.

ninety days but causes the flower to increase in size, depending on the variety. One drop of the formula should be placed in the cup-like recess left by the removal of the tip-growth bud just beyond the flower bud. The unopened flower bud will perform in a strange fashion, as within a week it will break its dormancy and begin swelling, and in some varieties expand and fully open its flower within a month to six weeks.

While I am unable to explain to you the reason for this magic, you can take my word that it actually happens. I hasten to say that all varieties do not behave alike under its spell.

A Mathotiana which would naturally bloom in March, will flower in November. And the Debutante, a tender variety, has little value when blooming in its natural season of January, as its flowers are easily nipped off by cold spells, but will bloom beautifully if treated with the wondrous chemical. Not only that, but both of these varieties will produce flowers at least a half inch in diameter larger with much deeper coloring. On the other hand, Mrs. Lyman Clarke, a late March bloomer, will not respond well and has even produced distorted flowers when gibbed.

There are more Camellias that respond than do not and therefore gibbing has become an accepted practice among Camellia growers, especially those who grow them as show flowers. The cost of the material is very minimal as about a dollar's worth will treat fifty blooms. It is normally available through your local Camellia society. It's a lot of fun. Try it!

There are, however, certain precautions relative to its use. Use it on plants that have reached semi-maturity, or have twenty or more flowering buds. Also, only treat a portion of the buds on one plant, doing a couple a week, alternately, leaving half ungibbed.

Never gib the same bloom twice. And in the case of flowers that become so large that they drop from their calix when picked, wire them for stability.

The gibberellic acid which is sold in small vials can be kept for an entire season providing it is kept under refrigeration. It is best to get the proper eye-dropper type dispenser, which measures one drop at a time. Your local Camellia society will provide all of this and demonstrate how to use it, which is of course most simple.

One of the most discouraging incidents in cutting one of your best blooms, gibbed or not, is to have it separate from its calix. This can be prevented through wiring without marring its beauty.

All that is needed is a size twenty-two or twenty-four wire, obtainable from florists, cut to eighteen inch lengths. Carefully cup the flower in your hand and insert two lengths of wire at right angles through to the base of the flower, then twist carefully around the stem. I prefer to wire it directly to the natural stem, although

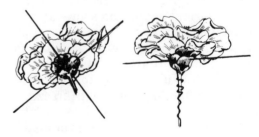

Wiring—a simple system to prevent flower-drop for prized Camellia blooms.

florists often separate them and wire them to artificial stems.

Camellias, in their multiples of species and varieties, lend themselves to any landscape. They are hardy anywhere in Zone 8 and can serve varying purposes in our gardens from that of ground cover to a stately evergreen tree.

No member of the plant world has captured my interest so permanently, and its growth in popularity was a constant goal of my entire gardening career. If I leave but one legacy for gardeners in Zone 8, let it be the love and continued culture of the Camellia genus—the true star in the magnificent world of nature.

scions inserted in split understock

moss covering protects against disturbance

Camellia grafting.

Ground Covers

To cover the ground, as the name implies, is but one of the major attributes of ground covers. The function of these low growing plants must be to cover without overpowering. For instance, Kudzu Vine or even English Ivy, although both have their use within certain environments, may become uncontrollable.

Perhaps the main purpose for using ground covers is to shade the ground and prevent other growth, especially weeds, from taking over. They also act as an insulator, keeping the ground cool in summer and warm in winter. This temperature control becomes most valuable in relation to other companion plants.

Environmental requirements must be carefully evaluated before a ground cover is used among other plantings. For instance, the use of any ground covers around the German or Bearded Iris would not be recommended, for it might induce Iris rot in this rhizomatous plant. On the other hand, Japanese Iris, its counterpart in the Iris family, would feel at home among some low growing ground cover like *Vinca minor.*

Few ground covers will survive the constant trampling given lawn grasses, a form of ground cover which can be kept uniformly cut and walked upon. A pure strand of Bermuda grass will never grow over six inches high, yet it cannot be considered a companion plant since it will take over most plants in its path.

Ground covers to be discussed for use in the home garden are a select group of plants which truly can be termed companions. Each will be carefully screened and given merits or demerits as the case may be. Ground covers may be either annual, living for one year, or perennial, living for several. Perennial plants are either evergreen or deciduous; the evergreens, of course, being more desirable from a year round standpoint. Since there is such variety in evergreen ground covers, and their preference is indisputable, I have chosen to limit discussion to them.

Bugle-Weed, *Ajuga reptans,* is familiar to most gardeners. It is native to Europe and is one of the Mint family. Evergreen and producing violet-blue or pink flowers in April, the plant hugs the ground and never grows over four

Ajuga.

inches high, with blooms six to eight inches tall.

One of the varieties offered in commerce is Bronze Beauty, with predominantly bronze foliage which becomes a lovely carpet among yellow tulips or other flowers. Silver Beauty has heavily variegated foliage in fine contrast to other Ajugas and *A. pyramidalis metallica crispa* has curiously crinkled metallic green leaves and taller spikes than those of the common Ajuga. *Ajuga genevensis brockbanki* has showy spikes of blue flowers in summer and *A. reptans rosy spire* is a lovely pink variety.

One main characteristic of Ajuga is its ability to grow in shade or full sun with equal ease. While it will flourish in most any soil, it prefers light sandy loam well fortified with humus to retain the required moisture. It should not be fertilized with high nitrogenous formulas since soft growth invites a form of crownrot, Sclerotium delphinii. This disease also occurs when it is planted on poorly drained land. Semesan, a mercury compound used at the rate of one tablespoon per gallon of water, will control the disease if affected portions are removed and the ground and surrounding plants sprayed.

Ajuga spreads through surface runners which readily root. It is one of our most valuable ground covers and is easily propagated. Lift in the spring or fall, divide into individual rooted pieces, and plant six inches apart. They will meet in one season's growth.

When given the proper environment, Ajuga will reach out even into lawns and choke out grass, other than Bermuda and Zoysia. While it creates a dense mat of foliage, it is not over-powering and will allow such small bulbs as Crocus to grow through. Therefore, it is considered an ideal ground cover for small gardens where refinement and texture are essential.

Silvermound, *Artemisia schmidtiana nana*, belongs to a large family of plants most of which are aromatic and silvery of foliage. This, however, is the only Artemisia or Wormwood considered here as a potential ground-cover. Growing to four inches, it can only be cultivated in dry locations in the full sun. Artemisia should be considered as a substitute for Santolina, which does well in this region under the same conditions.

Wintercreeper, *Euonymous*, is well known and suitable for a ground cover if carefully selected, located, and cared for. Varieties are most hardy and fast growing, not only along the ground as a creeper, but up the stems of plants as climbers although this defeats their purpose.

If you can control the growth of these ambitious plants, they will thrive where many others will not survive the varied soil conditions, damp locations, and even frequently invading tides. *Euonymous* grows in sun as well as shade, where it provides a fine cover under trees.

The small-leaved varieties are especially valuable, such as *E. fortunei kewensis*, which is possibly the most dainty of the *E. fortunei* group, along with *E. fortunei minimus*. Both grow three inches tall.

E. fortunei coloratus, six to eight inches tall, is a larger-leaved variety and is most valued for its autumn coloring which lasts all winter.

You have seen Galax in the pathless woods or at least in florists' designs with its prized heart-shaped leaves, four to five inches in diameter. It reaches its climax when the flowers appear in June and July, a foot or more tall in spikes. However, its autumn coloring, even in deep shade, attracts the most attention as the foliage mats the forest floor six inches deep. This is the type of ground cover that lends contrast to other acid-loving plants like Azaleas, Rhododendrons, and Camellias.

exert leverage to break roots apart

Root division—a better system than "cutting-through."

To thrive, Galax needs at least half leaf mold or peat moss and from half shade to full shade. To increase, carefully divide the roots in September and thus separate the underground runners.

While it is easily transplanted from the wild as divisions in the fall or spring, it is a protected wild flower, and illegal to pick. Only nurseries dealing in native plants handle it.

In its proper environment, the Dwarf Cape Jasmine, *Gardenia jasminoides radicans*, becomes a sturdy evergreen ground cover, ten to twelve inches tall. Individual plants spread to three feet and more. While in bloom during June and July, its fragrant blossoms are most delightful, perfectly formed, miniature Gardenias.

It prefers full sun and well-drained land. Thriving in ordinary sandy loam, Gardenias should not be over-fertilized. An annual application in early spring of half cottonseed meal and half bone meal is ample. Do not use over one cup of the mixture per well established plant.

Wintergreen, *Gaultheria procumbens,* is an excellent low creeper for the wild garden. The flowers are inconspicuous, but the red fruit, which persists through the winter, is most ornamental and the source of an essential oil used in flavoring. For anyone desiring a dainty ground cover, never growing over three inches high, Wintergreen should be considered. It prefers shade and will be found growing in association with mosses. While it will grow in poor acid soil, it likes moisture. Unlike most wild creepers, it is easily transplanted from the wild and propagated by divisions.

Commonly known as English Ivy, *Hedera* grows wild in Europe, the Canary Islands, North Africa, and Asia. The thick, leathery, slightly lobed leaves vary in color, shape, and even in size. As a ground cover it has no peer, if you are prepared to keep it within its alloted space. This fact must be emphasized, even when using the small-leaved varieties which are now available in so many forms. Many of them are Hahn's originations such as Hahn's Self-Branching, and Hahn's Variegated. Others are Manda's Crested, Maple Queen, Stardust, Purpurea, Buttercup, and Pedata, Caenwoodiana.

English Ivy is a valuable evergreen for covering walls, trunks of trees, and trellises. While it becomes overpowering through its creeping and climbing habit, it never becomes so dense that bulbs and strong-growing perennials will not penetrate and benefit by the insulation it creates. Ivy keeps the soil surface cool in summer and warm in winter and is of a density to repel most weeds. It can also be used for hanging baskets and is popular for windowboxes, enduring varying conditions such as poor soil, sun, or shade.

In addition, Ivy is an ideal plant to retain banks as it self-roots along the way. It propagates easily from just sticking sprigs in water, a cold frame, or even in the open ground in a shaded, moist spot. For ground cover, plant a foot or more apart because it will grow at least three feet the first season, one way or another.

It is difficult to determine what exactly constitutes a ground cover. Coralbells, *Heuchera sanguinea*, fall into the in-between category. Its white, pink, or red flower stalks grow to eighteen inches and are persistent for at least two months in the spring. When out of bloom, however, it forms mounds of heart-shaped leaves which are most attractive and persistently evergreen. If by misclassifying this plant as a ground cover we introduce it into your garden, you will be pleased and find many uses for it.

Coralbells prefer full sun but will survive in partial shade. Propagate by crown division and it will readily multiply. Set the divisions in October or spring, one foot apart in ordinary garden soil. The hybrids are far superior to the wild types. The Bressingham Hybrids are available from white through pink and Rosamundii in coral-pink.

A most noteworthy evergreen creeper, *Hypericum*, commonly known as St. Johnswort, is recommended for the small garden since it grows to only one foot. A dense grower, it will allow few weeds to penetrate once established. Daffodils and Lilies, however, will readily come through, and Hypericum is an ideal ground cover for them. It is sometimes listed as Aaron's Beard. The golden yellow flowers are most attractive although the plant is grown primarily for its clean cut foliage, which is blue-green underneath and dark green above.

Seemingly immune to pests, St. Johnswort will grow in most any soil. However, its foliar texture will be much richer when planted in fertile loam. It will tolerate some shade but prefers full sun for greater production of its flowers in early summer during June and July.

Hypericum spreads most prolifically by underground runners and can be planted twelve to eighteen inches apart. The runners will meet in one season. It may be easily propagated by root division. Cuttings may also be rooted in June by placing them in sand in a cold frame.

Hypericum.

Evergreen Candytuft, *Iberis sempervirens,* can be considered one of the best ground covers for the perennial border although it is normally grown as a specimen plant or as an edging. While it cannot be considered a rugged ground cover, as grass and weeds will penetrate its fine-textured green foliage, it is a gem for a well-kept garden. There are many varieties descriptive of its white florescence, such as Purity, Autumn Snow, and Christmas Snow. The last two repeat their bloom in the fall. There is also Little Gem, which grows only six inches tall in comparison to the others which reach eight to twelve inches. Candytuft grows in ordinary, well-drained soil, doing best in full sun although tolerating partial shade. Candytuft is easily propagated by division in September, cuttings in June, or by seed sown in early spring. To get quick cover, plant the seeds from six to eight inches apart and cut them back as soon as they are through flowering in April and May.

Both *Juniperus chinensis sargenti* and *Juniperus conferta* are fine needle-leaved evergreens, spreading eight to ten feet at maturity without growing over a foot tall. *J. chinensis sargenti* has blue berries and *J. conferta* has black. Both are most effective in the fall. They are hardy and prefer open land like seashore gardens since they originate from the open slopes of China and Japan and are resistant to salt air damage. It is best to use them among other needle-leaved evergreens such as upright growing Junipers and conifers like the Japanese Black Pine, *Pinus thunbergi.* Do not plant this type of ground cover with Tulips or other bulbs.

Junipers can be propagated by seed or layering, also by cuttings if a hotbed is available. However, for the average home, plants are best purchased. They are slow starters and can be set three to four feet apart.

Liriope is commonly referred to as Lilyturf. For some reason it was not used as far north as Tidewater, Virginia, until the fifties, although it was very popular in the deep south as a border plant and ground cover. Now its rich green, grasslike foliage is being used in great quantities and is not only perfectly hardy but most popular. One variety, *L. spicata,* flowers in August, bearing lavender spikes, varying in color through purple and violet. Some of the newer varieties are pure white. These blooms are followed by black fruit, which, in combination with bright green foliage, is most attractive. The plant grows to twelve inches including the flowering spikes. There are many new varieties of Liriope now available including *L. muscari variegated* and *L. muscari exiliflora.* Both have broader foliage than *L. spicata.*

Liriope's density will permit only the strongest growth to penetrate, and, therefore, it is not recommended as a ground cover over bulbs or among herbaceous perennials. It makes a fine

Liriope, Lilyturf.

border plant, especially near buildings where it serves as a transitional growth to turf, eliminating hand clipping or edging.

It prefers some shade, developing deeper green foliage, but will thrive in full sun and any soil which is on the acid side. For best performance, cut back each spring before it resumes growth. No diseases or insects seem to bother it.

Lilyturf spreads by stolons and also self-sows. Divide clumps immediately after blooming or in early April. A single division will increase in two years to a plant no less than a foot in diameter. Seedlings will grow to a matured plant in three years.

To some people, Honeysuckle, *Lonicera japonica* may be nostalgic, the sweet scent of its flowers bringing back fond memories. From the standpoint of its overpowering growth, however, its location in the garden must be carefully evaluated. Certainly none of the Honeysuckles are advocated for small meticulously kept yards unless they are used to cover a fence, for they have the capacity both to creep and to climb. For this bold effect it is invaluable, but should be kept under control by hard pruning at least once a year.

For large areas, Honeysuckle has few competitors as a ground cover where you wish to reduce the maintenance of grass cutting and walking is not necessary.

The Asiatic species, *L. japonica,* which has escaped cultivation since its introduction to America, is valuable under those conditions. It is nearly evergreen in Zone 8 and will overrun our native Honeysuckle, *L. sempervirens,* which is evergreen and not nearly as rampant, has orange-red and yellow flowers, followed by persistent red berries.

L. japonica halliana, Hall's Honeysuckle, has white to buff-yellow flowers with black fruit. Another species, *L. henryi,* is particularly attractive for its black fruit, and bears reddish-purple flowers in June.

Lonicera thrives in well-drained loamy soil. All Honeysuckles are self-propagating and may be increased by seed or by cuttings. Plant them in the sun or shade.

Creeping Mahonia, *Mahonia repens,* unfortunately has not been carried by nurseries although it does well. It makes an attractive ground cover about a foot high and is a favorite on the Pacific coast.

It prefers shade and a well-drained loam but will tolerate sun. While the foliage of this creeping species is not as lustrous as the larger *Mahonia aquifolium,* it has a place as a ground cover among broad-leaved evergreens. When used around other Mahonias such as *M. aquifolium,* three feet tall, and *M. bealei,* to twelve feet, it lends a pleasant contrast to the setting.

Partridge-Berry, *Mitchella repens,* is a dainty native ground cover found growing in most of our rich woodlands. In time it will make a mat two inches deep. In the fall it produces its best display with a crop of red berries which are, of course, a delight to birds, hence its name. It seems to delight in deep shade, snuggling around any acid-loving plant. This evergreen creeper, which gradually spreads by stem rootings, is not easily transplanted as it requires a sandy peaty soil and will not tolerate full sun. However, it can be successfully moved from the wild as a sod. Unless you are sure of giving it a suitable home, do not disturb it from its native habitat, as it is one of our woodland gems.

Partridge-Berry is not competitive in the midst of other plants so only use it if you are prepared to fight encroachment from other stronger woodland species. It will be a most rewarding experience. It is also frequently used in terrariums, where it puts on a wonderful show.

Dwarf Lilyturf, *Mondo ophiopogon,* is a small counterpart of Liriope growing to only six inches. It, too, can be purchased with variegated foliage. Lilyturf is particularly useful as a ground cover near the trunk of a tree where nothing else, including grass, will grow, as at the base of an old dense *Magnolia grandiflora.* Given any kind of a start, even among Magnolias' thick surface roots, it will soon form a rich green carpet. While it will not stand constant foot traffic, it is most attractive to fill the open cracks of a shaded flagstone terrace.

As with Liriope, it is best to cut back Lilyturf in early spring with a sharp lawn mower, set two to three inches high. It needs no spraying against insects and diseases and is not particular about soil type as long as it is well drained and on the acid side. It prefers full shade and can be propagated by division, although it spreads quite rapidly through underground rhizome-like stolons.

Commonly called Japanese Spurge, *Pachysandra terminalis* is among the top of six of the most suitable ground covers for Zone 8. It forms an evergreen mat under the most adverse conditions, such as in the proximity of the bole of trees. Grad-

ually and tenaciously spreading out by underground runners, it is not overpowering and is easily kept under control. The variety Silver Edge is a newer and rarer form but most attractive, sporting a narrow silvery white margin around each leaf.

When purchasing it as divisions, set it six inches apart, or from pots eight to ten inches apart. Pachysandra is not particular about soil as long as it is well drained. Preferring dense shade, it is an excellent plant around trees.

Moss Pink, *Phlox subulata,* which is listed as a perennial, is evergreen and spreads rapidly if planted in the full sun. It prefers sandy soil, well supplied with humus and well drained. It is a good ground cover for spring effect during April, but must be kept clean, as it offers no competition to strong weeds.

New varieties are much improved in colors over the original purplish pink, which forms cascading mats on wiry stems about five inches tall. Covered with blooms in the spring are such varieties as Admiration, a rose red; Alexander's Pink; Eventide or Starglow, blue tones; Vivid, a clear pink without a trace of magenta; Scarlet Flame, nearest to a clear red; and White Delight.

Lavender Cotton, *Santolina,* has become one of the most popular ground cover and border plants and is hardy to New York. Its silver-gray, evergreen foliage is distinct in texture and is used as a fragrant herb. If left on its own it will grow to eighteen inches high and eventually spread to three or more feet, although it does not propagate itself by runners, and remains a single plant.

There is a green form, *Santolina virens,* with yellow, button-like flowers for contrast; these same flowers seem to clash and detract from the silvery-gray form. It grows to the same height and spreads like the gray Santolina. When massed together they are most effective.

To get the best results from Santolina, set it on well-drained soil in the full open sun. It will tolerate drought; in fact, its only enemy is sogginess. It revels as a bank planting or in elevated planters where it will gracefully cascade.

From six inch plants set out in the spring twelve to fifteen inches apart, Santolina will meet and form a dense mat the first season. Thereafter, shear them back once a year, before or after their button like yellow flowers appear in early summer, as the flowers are not desirable.

Santolina, when well established, will control almost any weed growth, including Nut-Grass, and has no peer as an attractive ground cover for that purpose. It harbors no insects or fungi, perhaps because of its highly aromatic foliage. It makes an excellent border plant along the sunny side of a building to act as a transitional planting and buffer to the lawn area, eliminating hand trimming.

Santolina is easily propagated from summer cuttings after completing its spring growth. Insert three to four inch tip growth cuttings into sharp sand or vermiculite in the conventional method.

It is a shame that *Sarcocca hookeriana humilis,* such a beautiful refined ground cover, has not been given a more pronounceable name, or even a common one. Perhaps this situation is due to its rather recent introduction from its native Himalaya

Mountains. While it will grow to two or more feet, it stands close shearing. *Sarcocca* produces small fragrant white flowers in the spring, followed by black berried fruit in the fall. Only a few nurseries carry this ground cover gem, but it is worth acquiring.

Only suited to shade, *Sarcocca* makes a fine ground cover among other taller, broad-leaved evergreens. It prefers leaf mold or acid soil and is associated with Pieris of similar foliage, Azaleas, and Rhododendrons. *Sarcocca* spreads slowly by underground root stocks and can be propagated by cutting or seeds and by division.

Commonly known either as Strawberry Geranium or Strawberry Begonia, *Saxifraga sarmentosa,* an old-fashioned house plant, is perfectly hardy to Zone 8 out-of-doors, although not entirely evergreen except in sheltered locations. It is also known as Mother-of-Thousands in certain sections, as common names have a way of differing. It is neither a Geranium nor a Begonia although its foliage does resemble that of a Strawberry, although thicker. Its feathery flower spikes, from eight to twelve inches in white or pink, are interesting during May and June.

Strawberry Begonias will never overpower any plant or, for that matter, weeds. Therefore it can only be considered as a dainty ground cover, preferably in planter boxes or pots, where it will over hang. The plant increases by runners and prefers a moist shady location in average soil.

Many varieties of Stonecrop, *Sedum,* are available and suitable as ground covers. The most common one is Sedum Acre, which derived its common name from its reputation that a plant will soon spread over an acre. It is also known as the Mossy Stonecrop or Golden moss, and, being the smallest of the Sedums, grows only three inches high. It produces golden flowers among pale green succulent foliage.

Like all Sedums, while it will tolerate poor soil, it will thrive in better soil and is valuable as a creeper among stepping stones or flagstone walks and terraces. It will grow in sun or light shade. There is also a white-flowered variety, *Sedum album*, which grows about twice as tall. One of the several improved forms is *S. spurium*. All are readily propagated by divison or cuttings. If you want plants that will thrive under adverse conditions, consider the Sedums, a gift of nature which seldom fails.

Houseleek, *sempervivum tectorum*, is a fine companion plant to Sedums in the dry garden, deriving its name from the fact that it is frequently grown on tiled roofs in Europe. Also referred to as Hen-and-Chickens, it has been grown in American gardens for over three hundred years, after being brought over from the Old World by the early settlers.

It has purplish flowers and smooth succulent leaves with purple tips. Varieties of this species are legion and are available from specialists, along with other good species of Sempervivum.

Since high humidity is not exactly suited to Houseleek's well-being, provide a select dry location, where the soil is poor, gritty, and well drained. It can be considered as a ground cover only under those conditions as it will not compete with rank weed growth where rich soil prevails.

Flowering plants disappear shortly after blooming, but are soon replaced by offshoots. Sempervivums are easily propagated by separating the rosettes or by leaf cuttings in the spring.

Germander, *Teucrium chamaedrys*, used for generations as an evergreen border plant, grows to one foot high in rich soil, although it prefers a well-drained, gritty situation. It will tolerate some shade but prefers full sun. *Teucrium* stands shearing well and when planted one foot apart, will form a dense ground cover within a season. It blooms during early summer, producing small rose-purple flowers in whorls of four on upright spikes which are quite attractive. The plant is valuable for its neat, gray-green foliage and growth habit. The variety *T. chamaedrys prostratum* only grows to eight inches tall and is more floriferous. *Teucrium* can be readily propagated in June or July by division or cuttings.

Mother-of-Thyme, *Thymus serpyllum*, a valuable herb used since earliest time, is a most fragrant creeping evergreen. Because it grows only an inch high it can be used to fill in the cracks of stepping stones and flagstone terraces. This tough plant will stand much abuse, even trampling, once established. It has dark green leaves with white, pink, or lavender flowers in summer. *Thymus vulgaris* or Common Thyme grows six inches tall and forms small mounds with purplish flowers.

Most Thyme species like open, dry situations but will stand some shade. In fact they seem to thrive in poor, gritty soil. While they prefer lime soil, they will grow in our normally acid conditions. The addition of lime, however, will accelerate their growth. Thyme can be planted six inches apart from divisions for quick coverage or propagated by seeds which are very tiny.

Big leaf Periwinkle, *Vinca major*, while more tender than *Vinca minor*, is perfectly hardy in Zone 8. It is much coarser and the pale lavender flowers are not as pleasing as *V. Minor*. It, however, is one of the best ground covers I know of for low areas where salt tides frequently invade. It really has no place in the small tidy garden as it is rampant; nevertheless, where space is no premium it can be most valuable. The variegated form, so frequently used in flower boxes, is much more desirable not only as a contrasting plant but because it is not so overpowering and the foliage is more refined.

Any soil seems to suit *Vinca*, and it will grow equally well in sun or shade. I know of no insect or fungus disease which attacks it in this area.

The small leaf Periwinkle, *Vinca minor*, without question is the best known and most used of all evergreen ground covers. While a European plant, it was used extensively both by Jefferson and Washington in their gardens. Since that time, in many parts of the eastern seaboard, it has escaped cultivation, slowly spreading and choking many inferior plants in its path.

The species *Vinca minor* is still very popular with its lavender-blue flowers. Many new clones are displacing it, notably Bowle's variety, which has deeper blue, larger flowers. It spreads mostly through the expansion of its crown, whereas *V. minor* spreads by sending out stems in all directions and rooting as it grows along.

Vinca minor Miss Jekyll is a white-flowered variety with smaller leaves which grows closer to the ground. It is

not as quick-growing as the others but most recommended. All *Vincas* make excellent ground covers over bulbs.

Periwinkle is not overpowering and must be carefully grown the first few years until established. New

Periwinkle.

plantings from divisions should be set out six inches apart, or, from potted clumps, one foot apart. For quick establishment dig in a generous layer of peat moss or leaf mold in the top six inches of soil.

Ground covers have always been one of my pet interests, and it is with much distress that I see how little they are used in landscaping. Perhaps through this brief introduction, you will begin to share my enthusiasm for this important member of the plant kingdom.

Lawns

The most important single element in maintaining sustained greenery in the landscape composition is grass, and without a doubt it is the most expensive per square foot of any material that might be used.

After much study, I have concluded that Zone 8 is one of the most difficult areas in which to grow a lush lawn. At times I have been tempted to recommend Crabgrass, as it is certainly more dependable than the more cultivated seeds in our zone. However, there is one grass that does well everywhere in our zone, and though often discounted, Bermuda grass is the best bet for Zone 8.

It is ironic when you consider that we are gardening within an area which is perhaps the most tolerant to varied plant species than all of the other ten climatic zones. And we are right across the fence from Zone 7, the birthplace of Blue grass, where some of our greatest turfs are found. The simple explanation is that no matter how we amend our soil composition with lime we have not been able to breed a variety of Blue grass, or for that matter, any so-called "cool-weather" species such as Fescues, Bents, and others, that will tolerate the sustained ninety degree-plus temperatures that prevail during

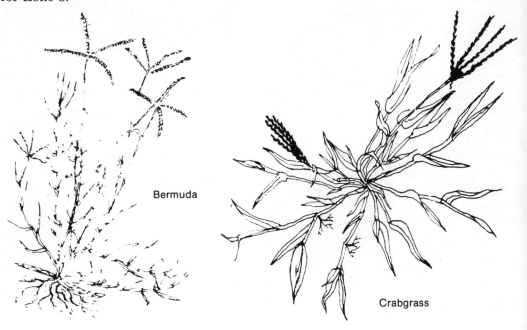

Bermuda

Crabgrass

July and August. Agronomists are working hard on this problem, but in so far as I know, no such break-through has yet occurred.

That is why I am not going to recommend types of grasses for all situations because the chance of a successful evergreen lawn is just too rare for the expense involved. I wish to quote one of our foremost lawn experts, L. N. Wise, who wrote a book on the subject and says in passing, "Mixtures are a combination of grasses, each having different strengths and weaknesses. Usually one grass is definitely the most desirable. The others are added as insurance to take care of special situations, inconsistent management, or lack of confidence on the part of the home owner in selecting a single grass."

I agree with Dr. Wise that we should select one single grass to do the job, and we can by resorting to our native Bermuda. It makes up into an excellent lawn if properly handled and will even tolerate approximately one-quarter shade. Under its auspices you can only expect verdure from June to December, as it browns out after the first killing frost and does not resume its active growth until late spring. This transitional period, however, can be bridged by over-seeding with annual Rye, as will be explained.

Bermuda grass is viewed with apprehension by most home owners as a weed, which it is. In general, we are not aware of the great research and breeding program which has sophisticated its adaptability to the extent that if you are a golfer, you have probably played on and admired its surface, both on the greens and fairways. This evolution has come about since 1942 at

the Georgia Coastal Plain Experiment Station, in Tifton, Georgia, a part of Zone 8 which has worked cooperatively with the United States Department of Agriculture and the Southern Golf Association.

Sprigged Bermuda lawn at Norfolk Botanical Gardens.

Tiflawn

According to Dr. Glenn Q. Burton, principal geneticist at the station, the best of these hybrids for home use is available under the trade name of Tiflawn or Tifton Fifty-Seven Bermuda grass. This hybrid spreads aggressively after sprigging and will quickly crowd out the common Bermuda grass. As it is a denser, more weed-free grass that sustains a great deal of punishment and wear, it is ideal for playgrounds and much-used areas. It stays green late into the season and suffers little injury from Winter Rye grass, resuming healthy and vigorous growth in the spring. Altogether much hardier than common Bermuda grass, Tifton Fifty-Seven requires less fertilizer and is more resistant to insects and diseases.

Sprigged Bermuda lawn
at Norfolk Botanical Gardens.

Tiflawn does not reproduce by seeds and can only be propagated by planting sprigs. It may be easily established, however, if the desired lawn area is properly graded and the soil well prepared as for a garden. A soil pH of 5.5 to 6.5 is best, and lime should be applied if a soil test shows a need. Before sprigging, broadcast fifteen to twenty pounds of complete fertilizer, such as 8-8-8, per one thousand square feet, and thoroughly work it and the lime into the soil.

Spring and summer plantings are usually best, but Tiflawn may be planted any month in the southern part of the Bermuda belt. Fall and winter plantings should be overseeded with three to five pounds of domestic Rye grass per one thousand square feet to help control erosion. Be sure to keep the Rye grass mowed to a height of about one inch to reduce competition with the Bermuda grass sprigs.

Secure fresh pure sprigs, preferably certified, of Tiflawn and plant them as soon as possible, but only when the soil is moist. Do not let them dry out or wilt. One of the best planting methods consists of dropping the sprig and pushing the basal end into the soft soil with a thin stick, one-eighth of an inch thick, until only the tip leaves are left protruding. Then remove the stick and firm the soil around the sprig by stepping on it. A twelve inch piece of one-eighth by one and one-half inch scrap iron with a "V" cut in the end, bolted to the end of a five foot stick, will enable one to plant sprigs in this manner from a standing position. Plant the sprigs on twelve inch centers for rapid coverage. One bushel or one square yard containing about two thousand sprigs, should cover two thousand square feet if planted on twelve inch centers. If planted on twenty-four inch centers, one bushel will plant eight thousand square feet.

Water the sprigs immediately after planting and keep the soil moist until they begin to grow. Weeds should be controlled if rapid establishment is desired and though exhausting, hand weeding is best. Mowing weekly at a height of one inch as soon as weeds begin to grow will help control them and favor the establishment of the grass.

For most soils annual fertilization will be required to maintain Tiflawn in top condition. A complete fertilizer, such as a 14-7-7, will supply nitrogen, phosphate, and potash in the ratios required and may be applied at the rate of five to ten pounds per one thousand square feet in March and as frequently thereafter as needed. A less expensive alternative is a complete fertilizer such as 8-8-8, which may be applied at the rate of ten pounds per one thousand square feet in March. It should be followed with an application of a nitrogen fertilizer such as three pounds of ammonium nitrate, uramite, or nitroform, or fifteen pounds of cottonseed meal or Milorganite over one thousand square feet at intervals of four to six weeks until the desired density and green color have been obtained. Use a fertilizer spreader or broadcast the fertilizer materials (as if they were seed) uniformly over the grass when it is dry. If applied properly and immediately watered, little burning will result from the application of these materials.

The lawn should be mowed weekly at a height of three-quarters to one inch in the sun, or two to three inches in light shade, and the clippings removed. For best results, water should be applied when grass begins to wilt. Although Tiflawn will survive droughts that will turn most other grasses brown, allowing it to do so will weaken the turf.

If your Tiflawn begins to show unexplainable signs of dying, consult your county agricultural agents as they can supply or obtain the assistance you need. As Dr. Glenn W. Burton says, "Good turf, like good health, is easier to keep than to recover once lost."

Other Grasses

While unquestionably the cultivated Tiflawn Bermuda grass remains the best for sunny lawns or those with up to one-fourth of the day in shade from tall trees, we must conclude that beyond this light tolerance, other grasses must be used. Kentucky 31 Fescue will stand up to one-half shade or filtered sunlight. Under conditions where the shade is created by trees, a lawn's maintenance is much more difficult because it is in competition with the trees for moisture.

Annual lawn fertilization.

I have, however, seen some beautiful Kentucky 31 Fescue lawns under the filtered sunlight of our native Pines, which are not as surface thirsty as most hardwoods. Under those conditions, Fescue should be sown heavily at its inception, using at least ten pounds of seeds per one thousand square feet, and never mowed closer than two to three inches high. It will also need reseeding each fall at half that rate to keep the turf from becoming coarse, which it naturally does as an individual grass.

With more than a half day of shade few grasses will grow, and you will require the help of ground covers, of which the best is *Mondo ophiopogon,* sometimes sold as Dwarf Lilyturf. An evergreen grasslike creeper, never growing over six inches tall, it will not stand constant mowing. In my yard, where I use it extensively, I cut it down to three inches once a year in April before it resumes its normal annual growth. Used as an edging in the woodland or between flagstones on a shaded terrace, it becomes a conversation piece of the landscape. And so far as I am concerned, wherever a practical and inexpensive lawn is desired, Bermuda and *Mondo* grass meet all the turf criteria of Zone 8.

I have a neighbor who over the past ten years has established a beautiful summer lawn from Zoysia grass, which also requires sprigging. The best of this type is known as Emerald Zoysia and was developed by the United States Department of Agriculture. The original species was brought from Northern Korea in 1930 and is an excellent grass for sun or shade. It becomes so dense, however, that it cannot be overseeded with a winter grass and will brown out by December,

after the first killing frost. This can be remedied by spraying its surface with vegetable dyes which are on the market for that purpose.

While St. Augustine and Centipede are extensively used in the Florida area, they will not be discussed here since I believe that Tiflawn Bermuda is the most adaptable grass for our purpose. Of course, we can stick with a Crab grass summer turf, overseeded with domestic Rye for winter greenery by just letting nature take over.

I have roughly calculated that the area over which we lay claim as a garden under Zone 8 covers approximately four hundred thousand square miles or the equivalent of 256 million acres, stretching 1,600 miles from Washington, D.C., south and west in a semi-circle to the Texas border and averaging 250 miles wide. After deducting for the lakes and rivers, swamps, highways and byways, buildings, and parking areas, and assuming that one percent is left for grass, we still have a goodly size lawn left of over two and one-half million acres. Therefore, there are approximately five million gardeners in Zone 8, each with some type of lawn to maintain. Considering all the expense and back-breaking work that goes into making a good turf, finding the correct type of grass certainly demands our utmost consideration; that is why I highly recommend Tiflawn Fifty-Seven.

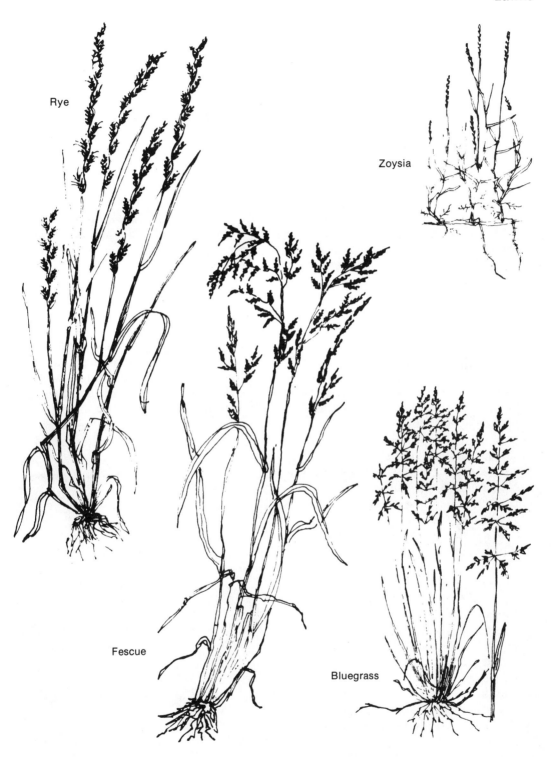

Lawns

Rye

Zoysia

Fescue

Bluegrass

143

Perennials

Versatile perennials, judiciously chosen and given proper treatment, will return year after year to brighten your gardens and lawn plantings with a full spectrum of colors from early spring into fall.

A majority of the perennials that look so tempting in the seed catalogs are adaptable to the climatic conditions of Zone 8. So there is no reason why you can't have colorful flowers in your garden all summer long. As a group they are somewhat out of their latitude and therefore cannot be chosen at random, although many will respond well to our hot humid summers. Often their success depends on using certain named varieties, as against others of the same species. I have tried hundreds in my own garden, and emerged with dozens, which have dictated my choice as presented here. Nevertheless perennials remain a very important, in fact, indispensable, factor in our garden composition.

We must remember, too, that while the term perennial means that they re-seed themselves and multiply from year to year, in this chapter a perennial will be treated as any plant that reappears after freezing back to the ground each year, regardless of whether it may be truly a biennial, as often the behavior of these two groups are dictated by environments. In fact, a few annuals may even behave as perennials, such as Snapdragons and Larkspur, although they respond best as biennials.

All the fifty perennials mentioned here have passed the test in my own garden, which proves that you can grow them, as well as many others, in spite of the fact that Zone 8 does not have a reputation as a perennial area. I invite gardeners who have had success with other plants in this category to write me about their experiences, as this is a valuable group of plants about which we should accumulate as much information as possible.

Achillea, commonly called Yarrow, behaves well in this area, especially the variety Coronation Gold, which flowers in May and repeats as a true perennial for several years. It will tolerate some shade, but prefers full sun. It produces multiple stems to three

Achillea.

feet which, when cut at the peak of its perfection, will keep their lovely coloring as dried bouquets for several years.

Althaea rosea, or Hollyhock, the old-fashioned plant of yesteryear, has been produced in many new hybrids. They are best treated as biennials and grown from seed each year. Consider the new Powder Puff hybrids from Park Seed Company that grow four to five feet.

Agapanthus, or Blue Lily of the Nile, truly a southern perennial, should be grown in containers or pots, as it blooms best when the roots are confined. It makes an excellent patio plant, blooming over a long period throughout the summer. They can be started from seed, but plants are available.

Artemisia, or Southernwood, is a sophisticated descendant of the western Sagebrush, and well suited for the dry garden. Not only is it a fragrant herb, but also is evergreen in texture, keeping its blue-gray foliage the year around. It might be classified as a dwarf shrub rather than a perennial. Some varieties, such as *A. schmidtiana nana,* Silver Mound, only grow to ten inches, but spread over a square foot of ground. Silver King makes a plant over three feet tall with a mist-like quality. Other types such as the well known Santolina are available.

Asclepias tuberosa, the Wild Butterfly weed of the roadsides, cannot be considered as a weed, but an exquisite summer-blooming plant that produces flower spikes up to two feet high in orange tones. They prefer some shade in well-drained soil. Even their seed pods are most attractive.

Aquilegia, better known as Columbines, come in legions of species and varieties, but those that stand our summer heat better are the large-flowered, so-called giant-spurred hybrids. They prefer a shady location with plenty of peat moss or leaf mold to send their roots for perennial behavior.

Alyssum, or Basket of Gold, needs no introduction: they are usually available ready to set out in full bloom in the spring. They will repeat year after year.

Aster, or the perennial Michaelmas Daisy, is a plant we can count on to set our fall gardens aglow with color. They can be selected in many colors and sizes to fit your needs. Asters are most reliable, and prefer full sun and ordinary soil.

Astilbe, commonly called perennial Spiraea, cannot be depended upon to repeat in Tidewater, except for the species *Venusta magnifica,* which is one of the larger of the tribe, sending out three-foot, light pink, plume-like flower spikes in mid-summer. It thrives in deep humus and in the shade.

Campanula will do best if you select the one listed as Carpatica Bellflower, which will serve you well once introduced as a dwarf border plant, even romping about searching

Artemisia.
National Arboretum photo.

145

for a comfortable spot in sun or shade. White and blue are its prime color ranges.

Coreopsis is one of the most carefree of the perennials, establishing itself even among sand dunes. The variety Sunburst is one of the better and most consistent.

Convallaria, known also as Lily of the Valley, is indispensable for deep shade, and should be started from pips, or small bulbs.

Chrysanthemums are so well known and grown that they should be selected for some particular use in the landscape.

Cheiranthus, or English Wall-flower, is actually a biennial, but best treated in this climate as a perennial. It can be raised from seed sown before mid-year to bloom in the fall and each succeeding year. Its blossom is very fragrant.

Dianthus, often called Pinks and including the old-fashioned Sweet William, are by far the best in the newer hybrids, which are consistent spring and summer bloomers. Queen of Hearts, a scarlet red, and Snow Flake are some of the easiest to raise from seeds sown in early spring to bloom on as perennials.

Dicentra, or Bleeding Heart, will thrive if given a cool, shaded area and planted in deep, rich loam. The newer hybrids, such as Bountiful, will bloom over a longer period than the older types.

Doronicum, also listed as Leopardsbane, has a beautiful Daisy-like flower in early spring. The blossoms disappear in the summer heat, but the heart-shaped leaves let it double as an attractive foliage plant.

Delphinium, in its true perennial varieties, will not stand our summer heat, but its best substitute is Larkspur, which should be treated as a biennial, sown in late summer to bloom the following spring. Larkspur should be sown where it is wanted, as it will not permit transplanting. It grows to three or four feet with flower spikes of many colors.

Echinops, better known as Globe Thistle, is best in this climate in the variety Taplow Blue—an excellent summer bloomer if afforded some shade. It grows to three feet and is excellent for dried flowers.

Eupatorium, also known as hardy Ageratum, will thrive and multiply itself from self-sown seed once established in the shaded garden. It blooms in late fall. The variety Coelstinum is a good blue with twelve to fifteen inch stems.

Gaillardia, or Blanket Flower, is a most adaptable plant with unusual flower coloring in brown and yellow tones. The giant English hybrids are favorites with four-inch flowers on eighteen to twenty-four inch stems, blooming most of the summer.

Geranium, as a perennial, is at its best in hardy Cranesbill, whose single flowers are popular in early spring borders. The varieties Wargrave Pink and Johnson's Blue are also most attractive.

Gerbera, also known as Transvaal Daisy, one of the best perennials for cut flowers, will bloom most of the summer once established in full sun. It produces Daisy-like flowers with the most varied colors on stems eighteen to twenty-four inches.

Gysophila paniculata, Baby's Breath, has its best performer in the variety Perfect, which blooms during

Gerbera.

shade and in woodsy soil as it resents chemicals in any form.

Hosta, or Plantain Lily, is valued in the shady garden for its colorful and variegated foliage. The specie *Grandiflora subcordata*, however, has fragrant flowers on twenty-four inch stems.

Hemerocallis, Day Lily, is perhaps the most adaptable perennial, with several thousands of varieties available. You can afford to be choosy in selecting your favorite colors and blooming periods.

Heuchera, or Coralbell, is a dainty late spring bloomer with eighteen-to-twenty-four inch wiry-stemmed flowers. In the variety Bressingham they are pink to red.

Hibiscus, a wild flowering perennial, is also known as Rose Mallow or Marsh Mallow, indicating its indifference to high or low land. The new hybrids like Southern Belle and Cotton Candy are truly spectacular, producing eight to ten inch diameter flowers on four to five foot stems all summer long.

Iberis sempervirens, the hardy Candytuft, is one of the best evergreen perennials to be used as a ground cover or border plant.

Iris, one of the better-known perennials, comes in many species and varieties which offer a broad selection for any garden scheme.

Kniphofia, or *Tritoma*, is also known as the Hot Poker plant. It is a spectacular summer bloomer that prefers full sun. It ranges from the dwarf Vanilla to four foot giants in the variety Golden Scepter.

Liriope, or Lilyturf, can be used in dense shade. It is evergreen in texture, and available in many varieties, such as Monroe, a pure white, and Majestic,

late spring and early summer. Pink Star, also a good one, has tiny double flowers.

Helleborus, known as Christmas Rose in the species Niger, and as the Lenten Rose in Orientalis, has spasmodic blooming periods, but the lovely blossoms are most hardy to the cold weather that prevails around its blooming time. It must be planted in the best of the lavender-flowered; both grow less than a foot, including flowers which are produced in late summer, followed by jetblack berries.

Lobelia cardinalis, the Cardinal Flower, is found normally in the deep northern woodlands, but it will do well as a perennial in Zone 8 if afforded deep, rich, woodsy soil and kept constantly moist. I grow mine with great success a foot above tidal waters, where it becomes a conversation piece when it exhibits its three to four foot crimson spikes in mid-August.

Lythrum, or Loosestrife, might be one of the better of the late-flowering plants. Murden's Pink with flower spikes to three feet stands our summer heat, especially if placed in partial shade.

Lavendula, old-fashioned Lavender, is still a favorite because of its highly-scented foliage. Varieties Hidcote and Gray Lady with wiry purple-blue flower spikes bloom early in the spring.

Monarda, also known as Bee Balm, is one of the few perennials to tolerate deep shade. Variety Adam, vivid red, and Didyma, pink with mahogany overtones, flower in summer, growing to three feet.

Nepeta, Mussini or Catnip, is a wonderful border plant with aromatic gray foliage and lavender-blue twelve to fifteen inch flowers that also are fragrant.

Oenothera, Evening Primrose, is a good performing perennial that produces three foot spikes of golden yellow flowers most of the summer, preferably in full sun and a dry location. It blooms in the evening.

Paeonia, Peony, unquestionably the best long-term perennial, repro-

duces for generations. It should be given a place of honor in the garden and left undisturbed. There are many varieties, all of which prefer full sun and rich loam.

Phlox, a family of herbaceous perennials, can be exhibited from early spring to mid-summer by taking advantage of its various species, starting with the creeping moss *Phlox sublata* to the *Paniculatas* for summer, the latter providing three to four foot spikes in most colors from white to deep red. All prefer full sun.

Platycodon, Chinese Bell Flower, an attractive summer-blooming perennial, is available in blue, white, and pink by using the Grandiflora strains. It grows to three feet, and is useful for dry sunny gardens near the seashore.

Physostegia, False Dragonhead, produces flower spikes of unusual formation in summer, growing to two feet. Firebird and Summersnow are two of the best.

Primulas.
National Arboretum photo.

Primula, or Primrose, is a large family of plants invaluable for shaded gardens. Those of Japanese origin are best.

Rudbeckia, Cornflower or Black-Eyed Susan, are among the easiest perennials to cultivate. Goldstrum is the most constant summer bloomer. Of the same group is the new Gloriosa Daisy, a hybrid, that can be treated and sown as an annual.

Rudbeckia Goldstrum.

Salvia farinacea is one of the best of blue flowers for the southern garden, blooming from early summer until late fall with eighteen to twenty-four inch flower spikes that can be used in dried arrangements. Salvia can be sown and handled as an annual, but can become a permanent perennial. It prefers full sun.

Santolina, Lavender Cotton or Ground Cypress, an evergreen with button-like yellow blossoms, is a most valuable plant in the border or as a ground cover. It can be had in two foliage textures, green and gray, which are often used together for contrast. It will grow only in well-drained situations where it is hot and dry.

Sedum, Stonecrop, a large group of plants that are most adaptable from low to high ground, comes in many varieties from the creeping Dragon's Blood to Indian Chief which produces large umbels of copper-hued flowers on twenty-four inch stems, all liking full sun. It is also valuable in dried arrangements.

Stokesia, Stokes' Aster, offers summer-flowering plants for the summer border, but also ranges in size to the two foot Blue Star and Silver Moon.

Statice, Sea Lavender, makes fine dried arrangements. *Latifolia violetta* and Collier's Pink grow up to two feet and are favorites. All like full sun and well-drained soil.

Solidago, cultivated Goldenrod, came along when it was decided Goldenrod did not affect hay fever sufferers after all. Many new hybrids sprung from the wild varieties, such as the English offerings Cloth of Gold, Golden Mosa, and Peter Pan, all developed from the American wild species.

Roses

Evaluating the Modern Rose
for the Beginner

The home gardener who is thinking seriously about growing Roses must realize their importance in the floral kingdom. A short history of the genus is most revealing.

Prior to the nineteenth century Roses were known and cultivated throughout the civilized world; in fact in 1800 there were over one hundred species classified. But it was through the loneliness of one powerful lady whose husband, Napoleon, was away trying to remake the map of the world, that the modern Rose as we know it today began to evolve.

One legend of this beginning would have us believe that Empress Josephine, although a beautiful woman, had bad teeth, and that in her vanity always carried a Rose in a characteristic movement of inhaling its perfume. She decided to improve this favorite flower and ordered all of the then-known species brought to Malmaison, her summer palace, and engaged the greatest horticulturists of that time, including Andre Dupont, Pierre Guillot, and the most enthusiastic rosarian of that period, Boitard. By 1824, these men and others, such as the famous illustrator P. L. Redoute, recorded the first comprehensive treatise on Roses and assembled the first great collection.

From this collection two Chinese Roses, Tea and Chinensis, were the ancestors of the modern Tea Roses.

Other species, such as the Persian Yellow and the Austrian Briar, or Copper Roses, were crossed to incorporate the yellow and copper tints which were so sought after. Regretfully we must tell you that these genes imparted that worst of all bugaboos, Black-Spot, into the modern Rose.

As these crosses prevailed over the centuries to create the modern Rose, the main categories that emerged and remain with us are Hybrid Teas, Multifloras, Grandifloras, Climbers, and Shrubs, and they all inherited that one foliar imperfection, Black-Spot, which in its wake has created an entirely new industry of "Rose sprays" and their efficient dispensers in the form of dusters and sprayers.

The incidental cause of
the modern Rose.

Therefore, if you wish to be a rosarian, you must understand the inherent difficulties. We are living in the sophisticated world of Roses which Empress Josephine started, and who would be satisfied to grow only the old-fashioned Roses of our grandmother's garden, which they claim never needed spraying, or *Rosa carolina* and *virginiana*, which still grow wild in our midst? Most of us are like Josephine, who wanted a consistent blooming Rose with fragrance, and although she never lived to see its fulfilment, she started the greatest evolution in horticulture.

The process still continues within the industry, as it strives for that perfect Rose which will never be attained because as individuals we hold different ideas of perfection, some favoring bigness of bloom, others preferring fragrance, while some, like myself, choosing their favorites for their ability to enhance the landscape.

A Beginner's Rose

The evolutionary process of Roses produced in 1932 the Fairy, classified as a Polyantha which perhaps excels all others in consistency of bloom; in Zone 8 it begins in May and prevails uninterrupted until Christmas unless stopped by an unusually hard freeze. It is hardy enough to resist Black-Spot or, at least, does not succumb to its inroads.

The Fairy produces clusters of tiny pink double flowers, each perfect in form, growing to a maximum of two feet in one season; after pruning the plant will attain four feet or more in diameter year after year.

The Fairy can be used as a border to other Roses and in foundation plantings or masses in the landscape where consistent color is wanted without the need for spraying. Its best credential is that it is still sold in great quantities, even camouflaged under various names such as the Pincushion Rose. You will find its true name in small print, which the trade requires.

One of the oldest of the Polyantha breed, Cecile Brunner, or the Pink Sweetheart, is still available. It originated in 1894 and is a counterpart to the Fairy in color, but has a climbing habit, reaching as high as twelve feet. We are indebted to such Rose specialists as Tillotson's Roses for their production and for the wide selection of old-fashioned Roses they carry.

Margo Koster and Carroll Ann are two varieties I discovered growing and flowering in the terrific heat of a New Orleans garden in August, while most other Roses were at a standstill. These are classified as Ranunculus and flower in orange-red clusters, growing to less than two feet, but much broader. For a change of color I would recommend Charlie McCarthy in pure white and Happy in red.

The next class of Roses in size are the Floribundas, which grow from two to four feet. All Gold has remained my favorite bright yellow, mostly because of its resistance to Black-Spot. Since it is a progeny of the Austrian yellow, the original breeder of this disease, it should have it but doesn't. It grows to three feet, with remarkable foliage texture.

Other Floribundas that will stand some neglect from spraying are the deep red Frensham, which are among the highest rated of the group and can be used as a four to five foot hedge, and Betty Prior, whose flowers are not unlike those of a pink Dogwood. From these trusty Roses we might consider the hardy shrub types of which Seafoam is a perfect example of ruggedness and adaptability. It produces clusters of pure white teardrop-shaped buds through the entire season and can be used as a shrub to ten feet or shaped into a self-standing pillar. It can be tied to a trellis and espaliered, or allowed to drape over a wall. In any form its small lustrous foliage seems to resist all insects and diseases. I warn you, however, it is most thorny, and as a hedge would repel any invader, friendly or otherwise.

Let us not forget in our evaluation of the carefree Rose those types that we might use as ground cover. Seeking from the most rugged species, we find that the Rugosa, variety *Repens alba,* is the best suited. After each fragrant white flower cluster has faded it produces red seed pods called Rose hips. It will form a dense mat by creeping out and re-rooting itself, and is especially adaptable to sandy loams, resisting the invasion of salt tides along the coast. There are many other forms of Rugosa Roses; some are tall to ten feet in pink and red flowers, and all have the same hardy characteristics.

In attempting to sift out from the thousands of varieties of the old and new Roses, those which are more or less carefree, we must invade that sophisticated entourage which captivates all of our fancies, the Hybrid Teas and Grandifloras, to find a few which are more resistant to Black-Spot than others. From my own garden of Roses, which is by no means sprayed regularly, I have observed the following Roses to be the most satisfactory.

John F. Kennedy's foliage seems to be one of the most disease-resistant, and its flower has a fragrance seldom encountered in white Roses. Its buds grow on eighteen inch stems and have over thirty-six individual, almost pure white petals. In pinks I would select Portrait or Miss All-American Beauty as its counterpart, both of which have the sophistication of the modern Rose. In my garden American Heritage is the best performer in the most popular color, yellow blend. It produces long sturdy canes and has outstanding foliage. There are many Reds, but for fragrance and all-around performance, Mister Lincoln remains in a class by itself. To round out the color spectrum Tropicana, which is an orange blend, meets all of the qualifications expected in a Rose.

I would complete my selection by adding another pink, although it lacks strong fragrance; Queen Elizabeth, a Grandiflora, should be included, because of its floriferousness. I know of no other Rose in that category which

Rosa Rugosa.
National Arboretum photo.

possesses its vigor and resistance to diseases and can produce such an abundance of blooms. There are hundreds of others that can be selected for other attributes.

Nevertheless success with Roses, no matter how hardy or disease-resistant they may be, depends primarily on two factors, placement and planting technique as discussed under Rose culture.

Initial Rose Care

Because the Rose as a cultivated plant has probably received more scientific research than any other, it is basic that we understand the reasons it is so special. First, most Rose plants offered in commerce are on a different root-stock than the named variety because it imparts greater vigor. The

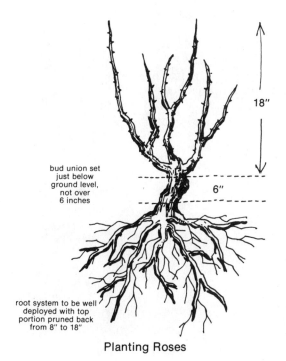

bud union set just below ground level, not over 6 inches

18"

6"

root system to be well deployed with top portion pruned back from 8" to 18"

Planting Roses

juncture spot, called the bud union, is clearly visible, and normally, when the Rose is purchased as a dormant plant, the root system below that union will be greater than the top, which has been severely pruned before shipping.

This vigorous and wild root system denotes, at least in part, the size of the hole which should be dug to accommodate it. The minimum size hole is at least twelve inches in diameter and eighteen inches deep, allowing the roots room to adequately spread out. Roses require a greater soil depth and more nutrients than most other plants.

Upon receiving dormant plants, which needless to say should be from a reliable source, immediately open the package and immerse their root-system in a gallon or more of water containing a plant hormone called transplantone. If the ground and the holes have not been pre-prepared, the Rose should be temporarily placed in the soil, a process called healing-in. This will relieve their in-transit shock.

Perhaps this simple procedure is the least understood in the handling of Roses, or for that matter any bare-rooted plant. I have so often witnessed such plants spread out and exposed to the sun and drying winds for as much as an hour, during which time desiccation of those tiny hair-roots has spelled its doom, nullifying all of the care they were afforded since they were dug from the original field.

The best procedure is to prepare the hole before unpacking the plant. Then immerse the plant in a trans-plantone preparation and use additional transplantone solution for watering in. The immersion of the plants should not, under any circumstances, be more than a couple of hours, and fifteen minutes will suffice. It is also very important to inspect the plant carefully and prune out any portion of the stem or root system that was injured in transit.

Since Roses remain in one position for an entire generation, it stands to reason that the root system must be given ample room for future development. Depth is needed for the plants to anchor into the subsoil in their search for coolness in the summer, as well as consistent moisture. Therefore, no matter how rich the soil may be, at least a pailful of good rich compost or manure should be dug into the subsoil eighteen inches deep or deeper, together with a cup of bonemeal as a reserve.

The soil which has been excavated should have at least another pail of humus or manure, together with another cup of bonemeal, well mixed into it. The plant itself should be held at the same level as the existing ground and the soil carefully worked into the root-system, leaving a saucer-like impression which will serve as a reservoir for water. This reservoir should be filled with about two to three inches of granulated Pine bark, which has been determined the best mulch because it lasts many years before disintegrating. While Roses are gross feeders, this will be all they will require on planting and will suffice for their first six months.

It is important to note that most of the soils found in Zone 8 are suited to Rose culture in so far as their pH values are concerned. However, it is helpful to have it checked to rectify any deficiencies and to maintain a pH range of six to seven percent. Most recommended Rose fertilizers will maintain the soil around that level.

Care of Established Roses

In Zone 8, Roses of the type recommended will grow for nearly nine months, which leaves only a three month dormancy. While we have recommended those which are most immune to Black-Spot and other diseases, all plants will perform better under a spray program. This should start in early spring just prior to the burgeoning stage which occurs from mid-March to April, at about the time the main pruning is done.

The pruning of a bush Rose consists of the removal of the weaker and crossing branches, plus the heading back of two-thirds of the remaining growth made the previous year. In this process you have eliminated many of the insect egg-masses which have over-

My roses get a severe pruning in March.

wintered. After this has been done the bushes are sprayed thoroughly with a lime-sulphur solution, which should be applied to the surrounding ground to eliminate many of the aphids that forage in spring as well as other insects. This should be done when temperatures are over forty-five degrees.

We emphasized the inroad of Black-Spot, a disease that attacks Rose foliage and eventually destroys it, for, unlike most plants, a Rose ceases to function without adequate foliage. Because this disease is in great part promoted by high humidity, it normally does not show up until after the first burst of flowers has been produced in June. Therefore prevention through the coating of the foliage with a fungicide such as Phaltan is imperative.

This means consistent programs of spraying with insecticide and fungicide every ten days is necessary from May until October. Fortunately sprayers and combination formulas are available, making the procedure less taxing than it may seem. Because the Rose is the queen among flowers, it requires such treatment. It remains for you to

Rose after March pruning.

determine the ingredients and applicators that will best serve your requirements, gauged on the types and number of Roses in your garden.

You will note that following a rain Rose plants seem to glisten with health, and yet we are told by some rosarians that water and Rose foliage do not mix and only promote more Black-Spot. They tell us that to water them we should saturate the ground and avoid the foliage. I do not subscribe to this theory, but do believe that water should be applied early in the morning so that the plants will dry out before sundown. This is quite feasible as an average automatic sprinkler takes only four hours to deposit the equivalent of about one inch of water, which Roses require per week during their active growing season. Deduct the accumulation of rain as noted by your rain gauge to determine what supplementary supply is needed.

Modern insecticides and fungicides, when applied properly, do not readily wash off and reach the most vulnerable underside of the foliage. Any moisture applied only tends to help develop the new foliage which is under constant formation. Since we have learned that plants take in much nourishment through their foliage, foliar feeding is practiced by many gardeners in lieu of more conventional methods.

So far as feeding Roses is concerned there can be no set formula prescribed, for it necessarily varies with the size of the plants and the product applied. Here again the foliage count prevails as the greater the leaf surface the more the plant can assimilate up to an optimum amount. What is the optimum amount? Normally it is the amount recommended by the manufacturer of the product, taking for granted that your plants are at the peak of production.

Like everything else, Roses can be overfed, and that is normally the rule rather than the exception. This is a detriment to the plant, as you cannot nurse a sick plant back to health with fertilizer and too much will result in the build-up of fertilizer salts, which a soil test will readily reveal.

For newly planted Roses the additives mixed in with the soil will give the plants all the food they need for the first six months. One further feeding in early September will help to develop that last crop of flowers.

With established plants the first feeding is recommended in the spring, following pruning and dormant spraying. I suggest an entirely organic formula consisting of a cup of bone meal and a cup of dry sheep or cow manure per square yard of soil surface. A month later, when the plants are just about setting their first crop of flower buds, a Rose food would be in order. Recommendations are made according to nutrient concentrations which vary with manufacturers. This may be from a teaspoonful per plant to as much as a tablespoonful or more. It is always best to apply these in liquid form, mixing the fertilizer application in a gallon of water per plant or at least by thoroughly watering it in.

Foliar feeding formulas applied with a sprayer should be carefully calibrated when mixing insecticides and fungicide. Be sure that they are compatible and since the spray schedule demands application every ten days, be sure the nutrients are added only once a month. I feel that varying

the diet of Roses by shifting from one recommended formula to another is most advantageous.

Because Roses do not particularly like high temperatures, which we experience during July and August, it is imperative that they never suffer from the lack of moisture, and that the soil surface be kept as cool as possible. This can be accomplished by keeping the beds well mulched with a two inch layer of granulated Pine bark, which allows the free passage of water and fertilizers. Feeding during those two months should be reduced to half, with the final application during September being at full strength.

Roses will prosper best in full sun with ample air circulation, which means that the Hybrid Teas and Grandifloras should be at least three feet apart with some of the smaller types two feet apart. Drainage is most essential, and can be best tested by digging a hole three feet deep when the ground is well saturated with moisture. Fill it with water; if it does not entirely disappear within a couple of hours you are in trouble, and better seek a remedy.

My final advice is to join the local Rose society for free advice. Attend the local Rose shows for inspiration and

Tiffany make a lovely bed of Roses.

never plant more than you can care for. Soon enough you will graduate into the company of those good amateurs, who are normally better than professionals, and soon forget about my guidelines as you discover your own individual methods for growing the favorite sweetheart of the plant kingdom. Just remember, Portrait, one of the Roses I recommended as carefree, was an award winner four years ago, and was bred by Mr. Carl Meyer, a pipe-fitter by trade. I dare say Empress Josephine would feel proud of his accomplishment.

The Fairy Rose.

Vegetables

One of the phenomena of American horticulture is the recent rise of the home vegetable garden, fed by an avalanche of new books on the subject and by the seed industry, which has the capacity to satisfy the increasing demand for new varieties and methods. I feel that the best contribution I can make to the trend is to describe an old French practice which can make vegetable gardening one hundred times easier for the home gardener, and more productive in the bargain. It has been my observation that good practical knowledge can save a great deal of wasted effort in both labor and material.

Some years ago a paperback book on postage stamp gardening captivated my attention because it brought back memories of my childhood days spent in Paris, France, where, on the outskirts, most of the vegetables grown to feed this great city were cultivated in small patches, mostly squares. The size of the area was designed so that the average housewife could buy its entire contents, pick them herself, wash them off, pay the man, and put them in her basket.

You can see the contrast in our modern way of shopping where everything is picked, washed, and packed within a cellophane wrapper before we ever see it. The Parisian system entirely eliminated the middleman: it was direct from the farmer to the buyer, and

My square garden gives me as large a crop as any row.

perhaps in some ways we are learning from that method.

Another recent book, *How to Grow Vegetables* by John Jeavens, more or less utilizes the same methods and calls itself a primer on "Biodynamics," the French method of intensive gardening, which I interpret as a new name for organic gardening. The basic principle is identical: by emulating the farmer and planting everything in rows, we waste much of our space in the small home garden, and the quality of the product suffers.

It is rather simple to evaluate the two methods by analyzing a popular vegetable, such as the Carrot. The farmer probably allows three feet between his rows, making room for his power cultivator which leaves behind a well-pulverized soil broken at least six inches deep. The Carrot rows are left undisturbed in about a foot of space and since the cultivator prongs are so set that a small amount of pulverized soil is added above them as a sort of dust mulch, they need little weeding and the ground is soon shaded by the tops.

Now let's see the way we do it: to save space we plant our rows from a foot to eighteen inches apart and cultivate our crop by walking up and down the rows. This continually packs the soil and is the main reason we harvest short nubby carrots instead of the long tapered ones we get at the market.

Now the French method differs in that the crops are sown in a small area, three to three and one half feet square, instead of long rows. The squares are bordered by various mulch materials and set about one foot apart, allowing easy access to each crop, which can be cultivated from the perimeter. I have found that patio blocks (2 by 8 by 16 inches) placed on edge, act as the best retainers.

The preparation of the soil is most important when using this method since the crop is so concentrated in a small area. For Carrots you should improve your soil at least a foot deep, which is actually a good practice for short-rooted plants. Do this by incorporating a bucketful of humus in some form and a cupful of dehydrated sheep or cow manure in every square yard of soil.

It should also be emphasized that each individual vegetable will take minor nutrients out of the soil, which is the reason that farmers rotate their crops. Since we are farming a small area so intensively, we too must remember from year to year to alternate the vegetables.

Believe it or not, in a three foot square area, an equivalent of thirty-six lineal feet of Carrots can be sown, producing a crop of at least one hundred and fifty plants.

The best way to sow Carrots is in seed tapes which come in sixteen foot lengths and contain two hundred and fifty evenly spaced seeds. Use the long rooted types such as Nantes Coreless, which will grow eight inches long in well-aerated, fertile soil. The rows should be placed three inches apart and thinned out before they are full grown. The small baby Carrots are a great delicacy and, if harvested at the right time, will increase your crop to three hundred.

Carrots mature in sixty-five days with sowing beginning March 15 and repeated every other month until September. In milder regions of the zone this crop will continue over the entire winter. Other vegetables that can be treated like the Carrots are Beets, Lettuce, Onions, Radishes, Turnips, Spinach, or any other small and leafy plants.

In planning and assembling this checker-board vegetable garden you will want to make sure that the taller crops normally planted in hills or rows, such as Beans, will not shade out the others. Beans of the bush type are still better planted in rows as they need hilling up, so I have suggested how this could be arranged in a planting chart.

Another advantage of in-square planting is the acceleration of the germination process and the better protection the seedlings get until they are well established. To that end I use burlap of the same dimension placed over the squares and kept dampened until germination has taken place. This will hasten the process by at least forty-eight hours, especially for those vegetables that have tiny seeds such as Carrots. Lettuce is practically impossible to germinate when high temperatures prevail and the soil is hot, but will respond well to this treatment.

Postage stamp vegetable garden.

With the treatment of the soil as advocated before planting, subsequent feeding is best done during their maturing period, using such quick-disolving liquid solutions as Rapid Grow. Peters is one which has various formulas for different crops. However, if you have a crop that you completely harvest, it is best to recondition the soil before planting your next crop. You need add no more humus, but if you used sheep manure the first go around,

change this to a cupful of cow manure this time.

One of the most frequent mistakes of amateur vegetable gardeners is overcropping. It often happens that the home gardener creates a garden too bountiful for his own appetite and time and effort are wasted in cultivating more than consumption can handle. For instance, under good cultivation practices, an average Bush Bean plant, such as Bountiful, will bear up to twenty-five matured Beans over a two week period, within sixty days of planting. Fifty plants, after thinning out to six inches apart in a twenty-five foot row, which is what the average packet will sow, have a potential yield of over a thousand String Beans.

Therefore it is most important to figure out your own needs and pre-determine the amount of space to use. Bush Beans should be spaced eighteen inches apart in rows as they need hilling for better growth. Plant them every two weeks, following the initial seeding in mid-April to May, until the last sowing in early September.

Another prolific vegetable is the Tomato. One plant can yield over fifty pounds of fruit during its bearing season, which normally starts around the Fourth of July and continues until cut off by frost. The Tomato, alone, illustrates why it pays to cultivate a vegetable garden.

On restricted real estate you will not want to consider ground-eating crops such as Corn or Potatoes, but rather quick maturing plants like Tomatoes and other bush types, which bear continually over the entire growing season. Vine crops are excellent for the home garden since their vertical growth is a great space saver. Four to five plants of a Bean vine, such as Kentucky Wonder Bean, when given an eight foot pole anchored eighteen inches under the soil, will provide one hundred Beans per plant from mid-June until November. They should be spaced at least three feet apart in hills.

In a climate where vegetables requiring a great deal of ground area are grown commercially it is more economical to buy them than to utilize precious garden space. Because of the high cost of labor many of these crops are now being sold to the buyer who is willing to pick them in the field. There are many variables that need evaluating before planning a vegetable garden.

My last recommendation is to study the climatic requirements of each type of vegetable, as some will thrive only during cool weather, while others like it hot. A perfect example of this is Lettuce, perhaps the most used of all vegetables, which over the years has been bred to produce varieties for all seasons, although a cool weather crop originally. As a general rule head Lettuce, like the Big Boston, will not tolerate heat and should be timed to produce during April, May and June from early sowings during February in cold frames. Leaf-producing varieties such as Oak-Leaf tolerate summer temperatures and should be sown from May until August. Thereafter, resume sowing the cold-resistant varieties such as Chicory and Endive, which can be harvested throughout the winter months.

Not to be overlooked are the crops which are tolerant to the entire ten month growing season of Zone 8. Swiss-Chard is one of these and can be sown in early spring for harvest fifty days later. By carefully removing the matured foliage it will keep on producing into early winter. This leafy and ornate vegetable can even be planted in the flower border, especially the newer variety, Rhubarb Swiss Chard. Another favorite vegetable, Okra, is produced on a plant that is truly ornamental and whose fruit follows beautiful flowers along the main stem. Clemson's spineless is a variety which grows to four to five foot plants.

After arriving at the size of your vegetable garden, locate it in an area where it will contribute to the aesthetics of your property as well as be open to full sunlight. It is best to have it enclosed since a fence not only acts as a support for climbing plants, but can camouflage a compost heap or fermenting container.

These fermenting containers, accelerators, will eliminate all odors and flies, and reduce all of your garden waste into rich compost within six months. Your waste is fed into the top of a three foot circular container, properly calibrated with vent holes and a top lid, and with an aperture at the bottom to extract the compost after it has been digested. One foreign model is on sale for less than fifty dollars with a money back guarantee.

You might also wish to include a cold frame at one end of your garden where you can start your early seedlings. They now have one that will vent itself automatically, opening and closing at sixty-eight degrees, which can also be equipped with a heating cable.

It is obvious that home vegetable gardening is a permanent part of the American scene and the only way to make it economically successful is through acquiring the necessary knowledge and equipment. I assure you that it is a lot of fun.

I believe that the greatest bonus derived from the use of home-grown vegetables is the satisfaction of knowing that along the way to your table, they have not been contaminated with some poisonous residue. But even that is possible if you have not observed common sense precautions should it be necessary to use some form of pesticide during the growing season.

For instance, one of the safer insecticides for edible crops is Sevin, a product of Union-Carbide, which in compliance with the up-dated U.S.D.A. regulations has printed in bold type: "STOP! All pesticides can be harmful to health and the environment if misused," so always read the label carefully and use only as directed.

The instructions also indicate how many days are necessary from spraying to harvest for safety from the carry-over toxicity. For instance, root crops can be harvested three days after spraying, but leaf vegetables require a minimum of fourteen days.

Perhaps the first spraying of a crop was a copper-sulfate and lime mixture used in 1878 by a French vineyard owner near Bordeaux, who became exasperated by the public picking his grapes while in their ripening stage. Incidentally the results proved that those sprayed were not infested by mildew while the unsprayed were. In this way, the famous "Bordeaux-mixture" was created and is still in use today.

We do not need to use this mixture in our own garden since the two greatest deterrents in the control of insects are water and natural parasites such as lady-bugs which can consume their own weight in aphids per day. Insects are particularly vulnerable to pressured water directed at them, especially aimed at the under-portion of their foliage, and if it were possible to syringe every portion of a plant periodically, few insects would ever survive, including spider mites, one of the most persistent and prolific. Another deterrent is the practicing of good garden sanitation, through composting all of the spent debris.

For those of you interested in more sophisticated methods of gardening I would like to suggest a pit greenhouse, an idea as old as gardening itself, and not as difficult to construct and maintain as might be imagined. I have discussed pit greenhouses in January, but wish to re-emphasize their usefulness in extending your vegetable season and providing an inexpensive means for year-round food crops.

While the mention of building a greenhouse in these times of energy shortages may seem to border on treason, a basic review of their function may change your mind. In fact, it may be said that greenhouses were the first constructions of man to harness solar energy, originating at the time he first understood the manufacture of glass and its magnification properties.

The first greenhouses were called pit-houses because they consisted of an A-frame superstructure covered with glass about four to five feet in height sitting over a pit of equivalent depth. In this way they were able to utilize both the natural warmth of the ground below and the radiation of the sun through the glass above.

Means of ventilation were added because on a cold day with freezing temperatures the solar radiation trapped within could reach sixty on a still day. To preserve this heat at night roller mats were spread out. During the cold periods it was for the most part the earth's warmth that kept the inside above the freezing point.

I speak from my own experience of years in dealing with such structures, the last of which I built in the old

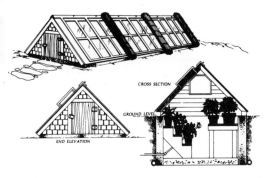

Pit greenhouse.

portion of the Norfolk Azalea Gardens. This plastic covered quonset-type construction, heated only by nature, housed tender Camellias and never had frost penetration in the entire ten years of its use. Neither was it ever covered over during the night, although the temperatures often dipped down into the teens.

The principle behind pit-houses is an outgrowth of the vegetable storage bins or cellars in use since time immemorial. In the climate of Zone 8 such greenhouses are not only feasible, but could set a precedent in the economical culture of certain crops which require cool house culture.

And solar energy as a modern concept has its origin in the greenhouse. Going back to the fundamental pit-house, the vegetable gardener can make a substantial impact on his food bill and provide a family with year-round produce that would be the envy of all.

The Growing-Harvesting Vegetable Time Table Chart

The growing-harvesting vegetable time table chart has been compiled exclusively for Zone 8 and can be kept from year to year as a sowing and setting out time-table. The name of the crop is followed in parentheses by the number of average days required to mature from seed in the open ground, the asterisk notes that it is best set out from plants either purchased or grown from plants separately, such as: Broccoli, Cauliflower, Egg Plant, Pepper, and Tomatoes. You will also note that Onion sets are recommended over those grown from seeds.

The harvesting period of various vegetables will vary from year to year, especially among those considered hardy, as are Beets, Brussels Sprouts, Cabbage, Carrots, Collards, Onions, Parsley, Parsnips, Kale, Spinach, Swiss Chard, and Turnips, which normally carry over after the turn of the year depending on the severity of the weather. With a little added protection, it is possible, however, to over-winter most of these, as would be the hardier types of Lettuce such as Endives. Please refer to the cultural hints for each individual type of vegetable.

Composite Vegetable Growing & Harvest Chart, Compiled for: EASTERN U.S. ZONE 8

Crops	Jan.	Feb.	Mar.	Apr.	May	Jun.	Jul.	Aug.	Sep.	Oct.	Nov.	Dec.
Beans, Snap (50-60)	★				■	■	★■	★■	★	★	★	★
Beans, Pole (80-90)	★	★		■	■	■	■	★■	★	★	★	★
Beets (50-60)			■	■	★■	★■	★■	★■	★	★	★	★
Broccoli (60-70)*						■	■	■		★	★	★
Brussels Sprouts (90-100)*	★	★				■	■	■			★	★
Cabbage (70-80)*	★	★	★			■	■	■		★	★	★
Cantaloupe (80-90)					■	■	★	★	★			
Carrots (70-80)	★	★	■	■	★■	★■	★■	★■	★	★	★	★
Cauliflower (60-80)*	★	★				■	■	■		★	★	★
Collards (70-80)		★				■	■	■	★	★		
Corn (80-90)				■	■	■	★■	★	★	★		
Cucumbers (60-70)				■	■	■	★■	★	★	★		
Eggplant (70-80)*					■	■	★■	★	★	★		
Kale (70-80)	★	★					■	■	★		★	★

Vegetable	1	2	3	4	5	6	7	8	9	10	11
Leeks (125-150)	★	★■	★■	★■	★■	★■	★■	★■	★	★	★
Lettuce, various (50-80)	★	★	■	★■	★■	★■	★■	★■	★■	★	★
Okra (60-70)	★	■		■	■	■	★	★	★	★	
Onion sets (30-90)	★	★■	★■	★■	★■	★■	★■	★■	★	★	★
Parsley (80-90)	★	★	■	■	■	★	★	★	★	★	★
Peas, various (60-70)		■	★	★	★					★	
Parsnips (100-120)	★	★		■	■	★	★	★	★	★	★
Peppers (70-80)*				■	■	■	★	★	★	★	
Pumpkins (100-120)*				■	■	■	★	★	★	★	★
Radishes (25-30)		■	■	★■	★■	★■	★	■	■	★	★
Spinach (50-60)	★			■	■	★	★	★	★	★	★
Squash, Summer (55-65)				■	■	■	★	★	★	★	
Squash, Winter (90-110)				■	■	■	★	★	★	★	
Swiss Chard (60-70)	★	★	■	★■	★■	★■	★	★	★	★	★
Tomatoes, various (70-80)*		■	■	★	★	★	★	★	★	★	
Turnips, various (45-65)	★		■	★■	★■	★■	★	★	★■	★	★
Watermelon (75-90)				■	■		★	★	★	★	

NOTE: (Days) required to maturity followed by * set out as plants
■ Sow or Plant outdoors ★ Harvesting period

Garden Plan for Temperate Zone 8

Postage-stamp section 4' by 4' each, made out of 2x8x16 Patio Blocks Laid on their 8" side using a dozen blocks

4' high plastic fence

Six Kentucky Wonder Pole Beans
2' apart; sown April 1

Six Tomato Plants 2' apart in wire cages; set out April 1

CARROTS
Sown March 1
Harvested by June
Followed by fall crop
sown before July

BEETS
Sown March 1
Harvested by June
Followed by fall crop
sown
before July

12" walkways mulched with pine bark

LETTUCE
Big Boston sown
March 1
Harvested by June
Followed by Oak Leaf

LETTUCE
Bibb sown April 1
Harvested by July
Followed by Oak Leaf

ONIONS
(Sets 1" in rows 3"
apart)
Plant in February for
harvest by July
Follow with another
setting
in August for fall and

New Zealand Spinach
(outer rows)
Sown in March
Harvested all year

2 rows of Swiss Chard in center

Dec.-Jan. sowing of early Peas along fence (Can be repeated in Oct.)

Inside fence row can also be used for Okra, Cucumber vines, and Summer Squash

Outside of fence sown in Larkspur in Sept. to bloom in June-July (Other annuals may be incorporated)

Rabbits do not like Leeks, so plant them outside the fence. It's also a longterm crop, 12 months continuous from Feb. to March

Such a garden can be under continuous cropping in this area by using winter-hardy crops to follow summer crops

166

Garden Plan for Temperate Zone 8

This is a scale drawing of my 1976 vegetable garden, 12' by 36', running North-South (important so that tall crops will not shade others).

—Frederic Heutte

Other small vegetables in succession (parsley and herbs)

LEEKS Sown in February Transplanted in April for fall and winter harvest

24" walks mulched with pine bark

Garden Gate

BEANPATCH

First sowing of Snap Beans April 1, harvest June

Second sowing April 15, harvest July

Third sowing May 1, harvest July-August

Fourth sowing May 15, harvest Aug.-Sept. Then repeat

Reserved for fall-winter crops sown in Sept. (Spinach, Kale, and others)

7 poles of Lima Beans sown April 15, harvested July 15 until frost; allowed to sprawl over fence

167

Gardening Basics

Over the three-score years that I have served my apprenticeship in gardening I have realized that success depends on the understanding of three basic factors: proper watering, pruning, and good sanitation.

Water is the most important of the three, and while we are most fortunate in Zone 8 to average around forty inches a year, it does not always come when needed, nor stay as long as necessary. So once again, nature will perform better with our helping hand.

Not only is water an important commodity, but in most cases, expensive, since it takes 27,143 gallons per acre to equal one inch of rainfall. Therefore we should be very careful in preserving nature's free moisture, and make sure that it is not wasted as run-off or through evaporation. Adequate soil preparation and good mulches are the best means of accomplishing moisture retention.

Plants generally require one inch of water per week during the entire growing season which can be approximately deduced from the growing days shown on the Zone 8 map. The winter or dormant seasons are taken care of through natural precipitation unless unusual weather conditions exist. The easiest way to tabulate a garden's water requirements is through a rain gauge because the weather reports of average rainfall do not accurately describe what occurs in specific locations.

Rain gauges can be purchased, although a straight-sided jar placed in an open area will do just as well. Each week at a scheduled time the rain gauge should be checked, and if the water is less than one inch, the discrepancy should be supplemented. To measure the amount of water distributed by your own system, place the rain gauge midway in the area to be sprinkled. Sprinklers with adjustable nozzles that regulate the water flow as well as the area to be covered are the best and are more economical in the long run than the cheaper models that waste water.

Rain gauge.

Pruning, unfortunately, is the least understood of the gardening techniques because no two plants should be treated alike, unless forming a hedge row. Therefore, it is important to understand the purpose behind pruning, and the general principles that govern the technique.

Most woody plants, such as trees and shrubs, cannot thrive beyond a couple of years if left on their own in the garden. They soon accumulate more top growth than their root systems can sustain, and nature's pruning never eliminates all the dead branches and twigs. For good health and vigorous growth all plants need to be open to the penetration, of light and air, and for aesthetic values this should be accomplished in the framework of natural growth habits.

Under our monthly schedule we should pay careful attention to the plants that have the most urgent pruning needs, such as fruit trees, vines, and Roses. But for overall success in gardening, pruning is a continuous practice, and no gardener should ever start out into the garden, even in leisure moments, without a pair of pruning shears within easy reach.

Pruning is a task for which there are no absolute guidelines, but it calls on using common sense in conjunction with an appreciation of rhythm and scale. Crowded silhouettes are not synonymous with beauty, nor, for that matter, a plant's good health. Crowded super-structures are havens for insects and diseases which are the only things that thrive in dark, poorly ventilated corners.

If we wish to create topiary or form hedges then let us choose plants that are naturally geared for that purpose such as certain members of the Cedar family, Yew, Ilex, and other small-leafed plants. The technique used to turn a shrub into a desired design or shape is shearing, not pruning, and should be used only if necessary.

Hedges should always be sheared with a slight bevel to give maximum exposure to light and air. And regardless of the time required in shearing your topiary or hedge, pruning out the dead branches and heavy undergrowth—a process called plucking—is still necessary.

Of no less importance in the overall management of a garden, no matter what size it may be, is good sanitation...a synonym for the compost heap. Today's modern contrivances allow any gardener to handle his refuse in a most elegant manner, eliminating the need for the old fashioned and messy compost pile that served up odors attractive only to insects and animals.

Compost grinder.

It is no wonder that litter-cleaners, compost grinders, and accelerator bins have become part of the modern gardener's vocabulary. Although a substantial investment originally, this equipment will more than pay for itself in labor saved. Not only that, but the convenience of instant products like recycled mulch make good gardening habits much easier to come by.

Compost makes good soil.

However, the main benefit of the modern methods of handling debris is the better sanitation it affords the garden. Few gardeners realize what a reduction in insects and diseases this constitutes, which will eventually be realized in healthier plants and less need for spraying. Nature dictates that cleanliness is just as necessary out of doors as in.

Mention of technology's latest contributions to gardening brings to mind some of the tools that have been around for years, but are still misused. And what can be more basic to gardening than using the right tools.

The ordinary hoe is a good example which comes in many sizes and types. The proper length for a hoe is that, stood on end, it should reach the user's nose. The square-tipped hoe is intended for chopping weeds or mounding earth, such as in hilling Corn or other crops. But for all-round weeding, the scuffle type is much more useful, because it is operated by walking backwards and you do not trample over the area that you are weeding. Several models are available, and I prefer the one with the pointed end, which is more flexible in tight places.

Rakes are also important tools, At least two kinds are essential to most gardening and lawn operations. The iron rake is used to smooth over the earth and break up lumps, and the bamboo one serves to sweep up leaves and fine trash.

Because the hardest work is performed by shovels, we should have several different kinds. The long-handled shovels are best for digging and lifting, but there should be a choice of blade sizes to suit various situations.

And in conclusion, let me emphasize the importance of the proper pruning equipment, that should range from a six inch hand shear to those long-handled types operated through a ratchet and cantilever device for cutting up to a two-inch hardwood limb.

So much labor can be wasted through the use of improper tools that the selection of equipment is equally as important as that of your plant material. Study your gardening needs and what is available in the market before making the first purchase.

"Il faut cultiver notre jardin."

Candide, Voltaire

Resources

The key that opens the door to a successful garden can be a local telephone call; it may be your county agent, your local Parks Department or the Municipal Golf Course, because information is what you need and it is available in many sources and often free.

The resources listed here include parks and public gardens, where you can often get permission to take cuttings for grafting, commercial and nonprofit gardening literature, and names of seed houses and nurseries which carry many of the plants that I have discussed in the text. The list is at best partial, but should serve as a guide for exploring other avenues of information. In closing, may I strongly recommend that you join your local plant societies because you will not only gain valuable information and advice, but the advantage of learning from the mistakes and successes of other gardeners with similar interests.

Parks and Gardens in Zone 8

District of Columbia: The United States National Arboretum, 24th and R Street, N.E. The mecca for gardeners in Zone 8, these 415 acres contain species of most of the plant groups native to our zone.

Richmond, Virginia: Maymont Park overlooks the rapids of the James River and includes 94 acres of flowers and shrubs.

Bryan Park Azalea Garden, Bryan Hermitage Road and Bellevue Avenue. The twenty acres include 50,000 plants and over six hundred dogwood trees.

Norfolk, Virginia: The Norfolk Botanical Gardens, Airport Road, 175 acres of wooded gardens include one of the country's best Camellia collections, hundreds of thousands of Azaleas, and many planned gardens in bloom year round.

Chapel Hill, North Carolina: The North Carolina Botanical Garden (Coker Arboretum), University of North Carolina, Laurel Hill Road, Chapel Hill, 325 acres of native plants in their natural settings.

Durham, North Carolina: Sara P. Duke Gardens, Duke University, 55 acres specializing in Roses, Azaleas, and Irises.

Orangeburg, South Carolina: Edisto Memorial Gardens, Route 301 south, 85 acres of moss-draped trees, Camellias, Azaleas, and other native plants especially beautiful in late March.

Sumter, South Carolina: Swan Lake Iris Gardens, West Liberty Street, 120 acres famous for a beautiful collection of Japanese and Dutch Iris which reach their peak in May and June.

Athens, Georgia: University of Georgia, Whitehall Road, 4,000 acres of landscaped grounds featuring the native trees of Georgia.

University of Georgia Botanical Gardens, Whitehall Road, 275 acres of new garden featuring a Holly garden representing the species native to the original thirteen states.

Pine Mountain, Georgia: Callaway Gardens, off U. S. 27, featuring 2,500 acres of native trees, shrubs, wildflowers, and perennials in the foothills of the Appalachians, includes recreation facilities and a 7-acre vegetable garden.

Birmingham, Alabama: The Botanical Garden, 2612 Lane Park Road, 67 acres which include a three-acre Japanese garden and a conservatory featuring 500 varieties of rare plants.

Greenville, Mississippi: Euclid Park, Euclid Avenue and Fifth Avenue, a planting project of the Laurel Garden Club.

Horticultural Literature

American Camellia Society, Box 212, Massee Lane, Fort Valley, Georgia 31030: Publishes quarterly magazine and Year Book, $7.50 a year, a must for Camellia growers.

American Rose Society of America Inc., Box 30,000, Shreveport, Louisiana 71130: Publishes Rose monthly and Yearbook, $15.00 a year.

Flower and Garden, 4251 Pennsylvania Avenue, Kansas City, Missouri 64111: Publishes southern edition, $4.75 a year.

Holly Society of America Inc., 407 Fountain Green Road, Bel Air, Maryland 21014: Three yearly issues of Holly letter plus annual report for $5.00. Handbook of Hollies, $5.00.

Horticulture, 300 Massachusetts Avenue, Boston, Massachusetts 02115: Published monthly by the Massachusetts Horticultural Society at $9.00 a year.

Horticulturist, Mount Vernon, Virginia 22121: Publication of the American Horticultural Society, it is received six times a year with membership dues payment of $15.00, which entitles member to other services including rare seeds.

Organic Gardening and Farming, 33 East Minor Street, Emmous, Pennsylvania 18049: A wealth of information each month whether you are strictly an organic gardener or not. $6.85 per year.

Southern Living, 820 Shades Creek Parkway, Birmingham, Alabama 35209: Excellent gardening calendar and landscaping advice for this area. $7.00 per year.

Under Glass, Box 114, Irvington, New York 10533: Bi-monthly at $2.50 per year. Written exclusively for greenhouse gardeners.

Special Sources for Information and Unusual Plants

Brooklyn Botanic Garden, 1000 Washington Avenue, Brooklyn, New York 11225: Handbooks available on all types of special topics for $1.50. Send for their list of publications, written and authenticated by the world's best garden writers.

D. S. George Nurseries, 2491 Penfield Road, Fairport, New York 14450: Specialists since 1894 in hardy, large flowering Clematis vines.

Laurel Lake Gardens and Nursery Incorporated, Post Office Drawer 9, Salemburg, North Carolina 28385: Specialists in Camellias and nursery stock related to their culture. One thousand varieties available. Send for their free catalog.

Lord and Burnham, Irvington, New York 10533: Specialists in greenhouse manufacture.

Henry Leuthardt Nurseries Incorporated, Montauk Highway, East Moriches, New York 11940: Specialists in espaliered fruit trees, old fashioned Apples and Pear Trees, also Grapes, Raspberries, and Blueberries. Illustrated catalog for twenty-five cents.

Stark Brothers Nurseries, Louisiana, Missouri 63353: Colorful and well-illustrated catalog. Famous for its many fruit developments. Established in 1816, it is the largest and oldest nursery of its kind in America.

Tillotson Roses, 802 Brown's Valley Road, Watsonville, California 95076: Old, rare, and unusual Roses. Illustrated catalog is $1.00.

Thon's Garden Mums, Incorporated, 4815 Oak Street, Crystal Lake, Illinois 60014: Specialist in garden Chrysanthemums shipped as root cuttings. Over 180 varieties. Free illustrated catalog.

Van Bourgondien Brothers, Box A, Babylon, New York 11702: Illustrated color catalog. Specialist on imported bulbs of all varieties, perennials, and wildflowers.

Wayside Gardens Company, Hodges, South Carolina, 29695: Many rare, uncommon, or hard-to-find plant materials. Wide range of perennials, ornamental shrubs, trees, vines, and ground covers. Illustrated color catalog is $1.00.

George Tait and Sons, Incorporated, 900 Tidewater Drive, Norfolk, Virginia 23504: Vegetable seeds a specialty. Thorobred Grass Seed a registered trademark. Established in 1869. Free, illustrated catalog.

George W. Park Seed Company, Incorporated, Box 31, Greenwood, South Carolina 29647: Three thousand varieties of flower and vegetable seeds. Bulbs, plants, garden supplies and accessories. Established in 1868. Three million free, well illustrated catalogs mailed each year.

H. G. Hasting Company, Box 44088, Atlanta, Georgia 30336: Flower and vegetable seeds, nursery stock, Roses, and perennials. One of the best selections of southern vegetables. Retail stores in Atlanta, Birmingham, Alabama, Lawrenceville, Georgia, and Charlotte, North Carolina. Illustrated catalog.

Thompson and Morgan, 401 Kennedy Boulevard, Somerdale, New Jersey 08083: World famous seed company of England with United States branch at above address. Free, illustrated catalog contains nutrient value of vegetables. Unusual flower and tree seeds.

W. Atlee Burpee Company, 300 Park Avenue, Warminster, Pennsylvania 18974: Flower and vegetable seeds, bulbs, roots, nursery stock and wide selection of gardening aids. Free, illustrated catalog.

Glossary

This glossary of horticultural terms is based in part on the *Standard Cyclopedia of Horticulture* by L. H. Bailey published by the MacMillian Co., New York, 1925.

Containing only those items which I evaluated as being encountered commonly in the trade journals, garden magazines, and non-technical books, it is presented for the benefit of the reader.

Adventitious-buds: buds appearing on occasion, rather than in regular places and order, as those arising about wounds.

Alternate: any arrangement of leaves or other parts not opposite, placed singly at different heights on the stem.

Annual: of one season's duration from seed to maturity and death.

Anther: the pollen-bearing part of the stamen, borne at the top of the filament.

Appendage: an attached subsidiary or secondary part.

Armed: provided with any kind of strong and sharp defense, as with thorns, spines, prickles, or barbs.

Ascending: rising up; produced somewhat obliquely or indirectly upwards.

Asexual: seedless; without sex.

Axis: the main or central line of development of any plant; the main stem.

Biennial: of two seasons' duration from seed to maturity and death.

Bifoliate: with two leaflets to a leaf.

Bipinnate: twice-pinnate; when the primary divisions are pinnate.

Bisexual: two-sexed, having stamens and pistils.

Blade: the expanded part of leaf or petal.

Bole: the trunk of a tree, particularly of a large tree.

Bottom-heat: the condition that arises when the roots of plants, or the soil in which they grow, are exposed to a higher temperature than that of the air in which the aerial parts are growing.

Bract: a much-reduced leaf, particularly the small or scale-like leaves in a flower-cluster or associated with the flowers.

Breaking: said when buds start to grow.

Bud: an incipient shoot; the rudimentary or beginning state of a stem.

Budding: the operation of applying a single bud to the surface of the growing wood of the stock, with the intention that it shall grow. The bud is usually inserted underneath the bark of the scion, and is held in place by a bandage.

Bulb: a thickened part in a resting state, made up of scales or plates on a much-shortened axis.

Bulblet: aerial bulb; a bulb borne above ground, as in the flower-cluster or a leaf-axil.

Bush: a low and thick shrub, without distinct trunk.

Callus: a hard prominence or protuberance; in a cutting or on a severed or injured part, the roll of new covering tissue.

Calyx: the outer circle of floral envelopes.

Cambium: the layer of living tissue lying just under the bark which is the conduit of nutrients in a plant.

Campanulate: bell-shaped.

Capillary: hair-like; very slender.

Capsule: compound pod; a dry fruit of more than one ovary, opening at maturity.

Catkin: a scaly-bracted spike with declining flowers, prominent in Willows and Poplars.

Caudicle: little stem, stemlet.

Cavity: the depression at the bottom or stem-end of an Apple or similar fruit.

Cion: see Scion.

Clon or Clone: a group of plants, all of which have been derived by vegetative propagation from one original individual and are genetically identical. All the plants derived from the original "Peace Rose" are clones, or of the "Baldwin Apple," another. Plants raised from seed, although they may appear similar, are not genetically identical and do not represent clones.

Cone: a dense and usually elongated collection of flowers or fruits born beneath scales, as the staminate cones of Pines; they often become dry and woody durable parts.

Coniferous: cone-bearing.

Cordate: heart-shaped.

Cork: the name applied to the outer impervious layer of the bark; often not a living part.

Corm: a solid bulb-like part, usually subterranean, as the "bulb" of Crocus and Gladiolus.

Corolla: inner circle of floral envelopes: if the parts are separate, they are petals, if not separate, they are teeth, lobes, or divisions.

Cotyledon: seed-leaf; the primary leaf or leaves in the embryo: in some plants the cotyledon always remains in the seed-coats and in others (as Bean) it emerges on germination.

Creeper: a trailing shoot that takes root in the ground throughout its length.

Culm: the stem of grasses and similar plants.

Cuticle: the external rind or skin of a plant or part; usually applied to the thin waterproof membrane overlying the epidermis.

Cutting: a severed vegetative or asexual part of a plant used in propagation; as a cutting of root, of stem, or of leaf.

Cyme: a broad, more or less flat-topped determinate flower-cluster.

Deciduous: falling, as the leaves of non-evergreen trees.

Diocotyledonous: with two cotyledons.

Dioecious: having staminate and pistillate flowers on different plants.

Division: propagation by means of separating the root system or rhizome system into parts; cutting up the plant into several root-bearing parts or pieces.

Double: said of flowers that have more than the usual number of floral envelopes, particularly of petals.

Embryo: the plantlet in the seed.

Ephemeral: persisting for one day only, as flowers of Spiderwort.

Epidermis: superficial layer of cells and underneath the cuticle.

Epiphyte: air-plant growing on another or on some elevated support.

Essential organs: stamens and pistils.

Evergreen: remaining green throughout the year.

Exfoliating: coming off in thin layers, as the bark of Birch and other plants.

Eye: the marked center of a flower, a bud, or a tuber, as on a Potato; a single bud cutting.

Fastigiate: narrowing towards the top; having upright clustered branches; united into a conical bundle, for example Virginia Cedar.

Fibrous: fiber-like; containing fibers or threads.

Filament: stalk of the anther.

Fimbriate: fringed.

Flaccid: soft; lax and weak; not rigid.

Flagging: wilting; said particularly of newly-made cuttings and recently transplanted plants.

Flora: the plant population of a given region; also a book describing this population.

Florets: individual flowers of composites and grasses.

Floriferous: flower-bearing.

Frond: leaf of a Fern; sometimes used in a sense of foliage.

Generation: period from birth to death.

Germination: the unfolding of the embryo; the start of growth from a seed.

Glabrous: not hairy.

Glaucous: covered with a "bloom" or whitish substance that rubs off.

Graft: a branch or bud inserted on another plant with the intention that it shall grow there.

Habitat: particular place in which a plant grows; such as a swamp, roadside, lawn, woods, ballast-hill, hillside.

Hairs: a general name for many kinds of small and slender outgrowths on the parts of plants; special kinds of hairiness are designated as setose, villous, comose, pubescent, hirsute, and others.

Heel: an enlarged lower end of a cutting left over from the older or larger branch from which the cutting is taken.

Herb: naturally dying to the ground; without persistent stem above ground, lacking definite woody firm structure.

Herbaceous: not woody, dying down each year; said also of soft branches before they become woody.

Hermaphrodite: bearing both stamen and pistil in the same flower; bisexual.

Hip: fruit of the rose; an urn-like or closed receptacle bearing the seeds inside.

Hoary: with a close white or whitish down or pubescence.

Hybrid: a plant resulting from a cross between two or more parents that are more or less unlike.

Immarginate: without a rim or edge.

Imperfect Flower: having either stamens or pistils, but not both.

Indigenous: native to the region; not introduced from some other country.

Inflorescence: mode of flower bearing; technically less correct but much more common in the sense of a flower-cluster.

Internode: the part or space of stem between two nodes or joints.

Lanceolate: lance-shaped; much longer than broad.

Lateral: on or at the side.

Layer: a branch that takes root and gives rise to an independent plant.

Layering: a method of propagation in which a new plant is grown from roots or stems that are still a part of the parent plant. **Simple Layering:** this method is the most common form of layering and entails bending a stem to the ground, securing it with pegs or heavy object and covering it with soil. A tip must remain uncovered to allow circulation. The underside of the stem is often scraped or bruised in some way to accelerate root formation.

Leaflet: one part of a compound leaf; secondary leaf.

Leaf-Stalk: the stem of a leaf; petiole; foot-stalk.

Legume: simple pericarp (the ripened ovary).

Lobe: any part or segment of an organ; specifically a part of petal, calyx, or leaf that represents a division to about the middle.

Midrib: the main rib of a leaf or leaf-like part.

Monoecious: staminate and pistillate flowers on the same plant.

Mule: an odd word for a cross, particularly between different species; hybrid; cross-breed.

Mutant: a plant with genetic characteristics that differ from those of the parents.

Mycelium: vegetative part of a fungus, composed of threads or thready tissue.

Mychoriza: process by which plant produces its own nutrients.

Node: a joint where a leaf is borne or may be borne; also incorrectly the space between two joints, which is properly an internode.

Nucleus: the kernel of a seed; the central denser structure of a cell.

Nut: a one-celled and one-seeded hard and bony fruit, which does not open to discharge its seeds.

Obconical: inversely conical; cone attached at the small point.

Oblanceolate: inversely lanceolate; with the broadest part of a lance-shaped body away from the point of attachment.

Obtuse: blunt, rounded.

Ovary: ovule-bearing part of a pistil.

Ovule: the body which after fertilization becomes the seed.

Palmate: lobed or divided in a palm-like or hand-like fashion.

Panicle: a branching raceme; flower-cluster in which the branches are racemose.

Parasitic: growing and living on or in another organism.

Pedicle: stem of one flower in a cluster.

Peduncle: stem of a flower-cluster or of

a solitary flower.

Perennial: of three or more seasons' duration.

Perianth: the floral envelope considered together.

Persistent: remaining attached; not falling off.

Petal: one of the separate leaves of a corolla.

Petiole: leaf-stalk.

Pinnate: feather-formed: with leaflets of a compound leaf placed on either side.

Pip: a perpendicular or upright small root stock used in propagation as of Lily-of-the-Valley.

Pistil: the ovule-bearing and seed-bearing female organ.

Pistillate: having pistils and no stamens; female.

Pollen: spores or grains borne by the anther, containing the male element.

Pollination: the mechanical or physical operation of transferring pollen from stamen to pistil.

Prickle: a small and weak spine-like body borne irregularly on the bark or epidermis.

Procumbent: trailing or lying flat, but not rooting.

Pubescent: covered with short, soft hairs; downy.

Raceme: simple elongated indeterminate cluster with stalked flowers.

Recurved: bent or curved downward or backward.

Reflexed: abruptly recurved or bent downward or backward.

Rhizome: underground stem; root stock.

Rib: in a leaf or similar organ, the primary vein.

Rootstock: subterranean stem; rhizome.

Rudimentary: incomplete: very little developed.

Runner: a slender trailing shoot taking root at the nodes.

Sap: The watery contents of a plant.

Scale: a name given to many kinds of small, mostly dry and appressed leaves or bracts.

Scape: leafless peduncle arising from the ground.

Scion: the bud or branch used in grafting.

Seed: the ripened ovule.

Seedling: a young plant raised from seed.

Sepal: one of the separate leaves of a calyx.

Shoot: a new plant from the root of the old plant.

Shrub: a woody plant that remains low and produces shoots or trunks from the base.

Slip: a softwood cutting "slipped" off or pulled off.

Spathe: the bract or leaf surrounding a flower-cluster, sometimes colored and flower-like, as in the Calla.

Spike: compact, more or less simple, indeterminate, mostly elongated cluster, with flowers.

Spit: term used by gardeners to note the depth which is reached by thrusting a spade in the ground.

Spore: a simple reproductive body, usually composed of a single detached cell.

Sport: a sudden variation from type and habit of growth; botanists call sports "mutants."

Stamen: the pollen-bearing or "male" organ.

Staminate: having stamens and no pistils; male.

Stem: the main axis of a plant; leaf-bearing and flower-bearing, as distinguished from the root-bearing axis.

Sterile Flower: without pistils.

Stigma: part of the pistil that recreates the pollen.

Stipe: the stalk of a pistil or other small organ.

Stock: the part on which the scion is grafted.

Stolon: a shoot that bends to the ground and takes root; more commonly, a horizontal stem at or below surface of the ground that gives rise to a new plant at its tip.

Stratification: the operation or method of burying seeds to keep them fresh and to soften their outer coverings, or to expose them without injury to frost, that they may be more readily and successfully used in propagation.

Style: more or less elongated part of the pistil between the ovary and the stigma.

Succulent: juicy; fleshy; soft and thickened in texture.

Sucker: a shoot arising from the roots or beneath the surface of the ground. Also used to described shoots that arise from buds located anywhere along stem of the plant.

Tap-Root: a strong, nearly perpendicular main root that carries the plant axis straight to the ground, all the other roots being secondary to it, rather than branching equally or diversely at the crown.

Tendril: a rotating or twisting thread-like process or extension by which a plant grasps an object and clings to it for support.

Tomentose: densely wooly or pubescent, with matted soft wool-like hairiness.

Tree: a woody plant that produces one main trunk and a more or less distinct and elevated head.

Trifoliate: having three leaves.

Tuber: a short congested part: usually defined as subterranean (as of a rootstock), although this is not essential.

Umbel: indeterminate cluster with branches or rays arising from a common point and about equal in length, resembling framework of umbrella.

Vascular: with vessels or ducts, or relating to them.

Vein: a branch of the evident woody framework of a leaf or similar organ.

Watersprout: a strong rapid-growing adventitious shoot in a tree-top or bush (normally the aftermath of severe pruning).

Wort: old word for a plant or herb; now used only in combination as: Motherwort, Spiderwort, Liverwort.

Index

L

Laburnum cytisus 58
Lace bug 106
Lady Clare 16
Lagerstoemia indica 65
Larkspur 77, 95-96, 146
Latifolia violetta 149
Laurel
  Alexandrian 78
  Mountain 51
  Poets 78
Lavender 148
  Cotton 60, 134, 149
  Sea 149
Lavendula 148
Lawns 138-143
  fertilization 33
  July 70
  weed control 33
layering 15
leaf gall 107
Lenten Rose 17, 147
Leopardsbane 146
Lettuce 46, 161
Leucojum vernum 26
Ligustrum
  lucidum 49
  coriaceum 49
Lilac 40
  Summer 68
Lily 63, 64
  Crinum 75
  Day 63, 147
  Easter 63
  Ginger 74-75
  of the Nile, Blue 145
  -of-the-Valley 49, 146
  Plantain 147
  Regale 63
Lilyturf 72, 132-133, 147-148
  Dwarf 134, 142
Lime Tree 67
Linden 67
Liriodendron tulipifera 48
Liriope, Liriope 72, 132-33, 147-148
  muscari 72
  exiliflora 132
  variegated 132
  spicata 132
Lobelia, Lobelia 96
  cardinalis 72, 148
Loblolly
  Bay 56-57
  Pine 34
Locust 67
Lonicera
  henryi 133
  japonica 133

halliana 133
sempervirens 133
tatarica 72
Loosestrife 148
Loquat 81
Lusterleaf Holly 12-13, 86
Lycoris, Lycoris 75
  squamigera 75
Lythrum 148

M

Magnolia, Magnolia 27, 47-48
  Dr. Merrill 27
  grandiflora 47
  exoniensis 47
  stellata 27
  soulangeana 27
  nigra 27
  Sweetbay 58
  virginiana 58, 109
Mahonia, Mahonia
  aquifolium 109, 133
  bealei 133
  Creeping 133
  repens 133
Maidenhair
  Fern 72
  Tree 67
Malus 29
Maple 67
  Paperbark 67
March 25-34
Marigold 64, 96
Marsh Mallow 68, 147
Matthiola 26
May 47-55
Meratia praecox 21
mertensia virginica 53
Michaelmas Daisy 145
micro-climate 18
Mimosa 59
Mitchella repens 133
miten 23
  See Spider mite
Mock Orange 35, 50
Monarda 148
Monbretia 46, 75
Mondo ophiopogon 35, 85, 134, 142
Morning Glory 96
Moss Pink 134
Mother-of-Thyme 136
Mountain Laurel 51
Mulch 71, 84
  Azalea 104
Mum, see Chrysanthemum
Muscari plumosum album 26
Mussini 148

PLANT HARDINESS
FOR ZONE 8-A
AND 8-B

Fred Heutte's
Gardening in the Tempe

Physical area covered equals 1
Washington, D.C., to Texas bord
tinues west, presenting ecolog
covered by this book.) Average V
Total area: 400,000 square miles.

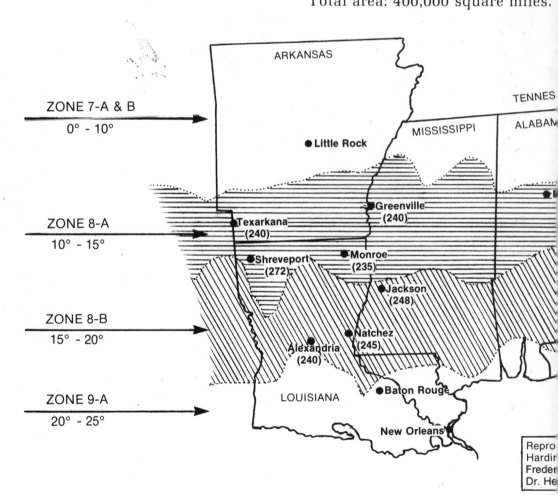

ARKANSAS

TENNES

MISSISSIPPI   ALABAM

●Little Rock

ZONE 7-A & B

0° - 10°

●Greenville
(240)

ZONE 8-A

10° - 15°

●Texarkana
(240)

●Shreveport   ●Monroe
(272)   (235)

●Jackson
(248)

ZONE 8-B

15° - 20°

●Natchez
(245)

●Alexandria
(240)

ZONE 9-A

20° - 25°

LOUISIANA   ●Baton Rouge

New Orleans